# How to Teach Spelling Without Going Crazy

by Cheryl L. Callighan
illustrated by Marilynn Barr

This book is dedicated to all those teachers
who were so willing to share their knowledge and experience.

Publisher: Roberta Suid
Copy Editor: Carol Whiteley
Design and Production: MGB Press
Cover Design: Dana Mardaga



Online address: MMBooks@aol.com
Web address: www.mondaymorningbooks.com

For a complete catalog, write to the address above.

ISBN1-57612-80-5
Printed in the United States of America
9 8 7 6 5 4 3 2 1

# CONTENTS

**SPELLING DEMONS**

# Introduction

- There isn't enough time.
- The children just want to use spell-checking programs on their computers.
- Our curriculum is whole language based.
- It should be taught in the lower grades.

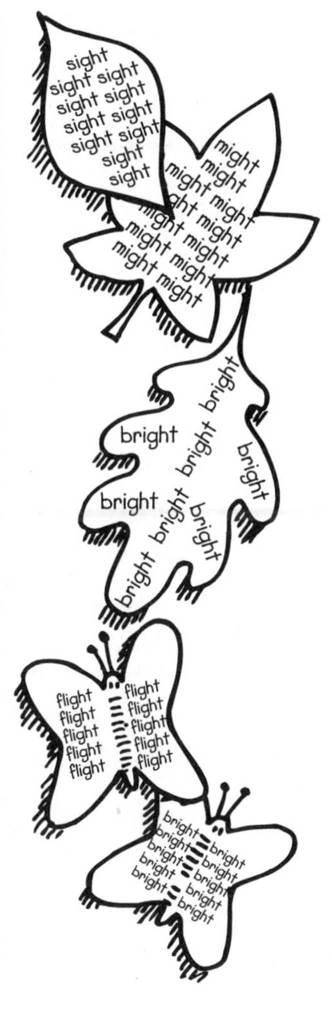


All of these are common laments when it comes to the subject of teaching spelling in the middle school. But spelling is important! In fact, it could be viewed as the foundation for all other forms of communication. Spelling is not just an isolated subject. Students must use spelling in every subject area. In addition, a firm knowledge of spelling can help promote reading ability. And once a child understands word families, patterns, prefixes, and suffixes, he or she is more able to grasp word analysis. As confidence in working with words increases, student confidence in other areas will grow as well.

While computer spell-checking programs are helpful, they are not foolproof. Spelling is still a very necessary skill. For example, spell-checkers will not let students know that they typed "wood" when they meant to write "would." It also doesn't alert users to a change in one or two letters; imagine spelling the word "invisible" when you wanted to say "invincible." The computer does not pick up subtle differences, such as that between "dessert" and "desert." And even if the program does point out an error, it may make suggestions for replacement but may not provide the user with the correct spelling of the original word.

Whole language curriculums do not exclude the teaching of spelling; spelling needs to be integrated into the program. Students gradually must become more responsible for using correctly spelled words in their writing. Spelling should always count on the final copy of a written assignments. And even if your program frowns on using spelling lists, you can still use activities to promote spelling skills and insist on the transference of those skills to other language arts venues.

Learning to spell well takes practice. It cannot be taught by rote memory alone. Even if a child receives an outstanding grade on a spelling test, he or she may not have truly mastered the spelling of those words. Correctly spelled words will not simply show up on children's papers if they have not learned some of the basic spelling and phonetic rules. A knowledge of those rules will help students make the right decision when they are faced with spelling choices. In addition, putting the rules into action will help build students' visual memory of words. Providing a combination of rules and practice will help build confident and accurate spellers.

The English language is complex and confusing, and it takes time to master it. In the early grades, students need to gain a strong phonetic knowledge for simple spelling. As they progress through the middle grades, they can handle more complex spelling concepts. Each year students should be given more techniques with which to cope with our demanding language.

This book contains a wide variety of activities to help you teach spelling without going crazy. It is divided into the following sections:

**The Diverse Classroom**—This section contains information about how to focus on students' learning styles, tips about individualizing programs, and adaptive techniques for dealing with special needs.

**Classroom Management**—In this section you'll find classroom management techniques, how to develop spelling bulletin boards, and suggestions for weekly plans. You'll also find helpful hints to assist you in understanding why your students are misspelling words.

**General Activities**—The activities include a wide array of spelling lessons that can be used with almost any existing list of words. The activities strive to incorporate all three learning styles (see next page) and include many environment-friendly projects.

**Topic-Specific Activities**—Here you'll find activities and word lists related to specific concepts, such as spelling rules, prefixes and suffixes, and homophones.

**Spelling Demons**—This part of the book provides techniques for coping with these fiends, plus a list of commonly misspelled words and spelling demons.

# THE DIVERSE CLASSROOM

## LEARNING STYLES

A classroom full of students is home to many different learning styles. These styles tend to fall into three main modalities: auditory, tactile, and visual. Students learn best when information is presented in a manner that coincides with their strongest learning mode. Of course, children never divide themselves into neat little categories. Many students need information presented in a combination of ways in order to understand to the best of their ability.

The activities in this book present lessons that work with a variety of learning styles. Children will learn from activities presented through their strongest learning mode but will also develop additional skills as they work with lessons presented through other techniques. Traditional spelling lessons that, week after week, have students writing words five times each on notebook paper and using each word in a sentence barely stimulate a tactile learner, bore the visual learner, and leave the auditory learner out in the cold. Presenting a variety of the activities in this book will help all types of learners remember the spelling words that they are practicing, and cover all the bases. Adjust your plans to meet the styles of your students.

To determine a student's best learning mode, start by asking the student his or her opinion. Even at a young age, students can verbalize their learning preferences. They will tell you, "I learn best by writing things down" or "I understand instructions well if I hear them." You can also consult the list of learning-style characteristics that follow to help you get a sense of which style will most benefit a specific learner. Keep in mind, however, that no one student will exactly fit a particular category.

## Auditory Learner

- Is a good listener
- Cues into the soundtrack of a film
- Understands oral directions with little difficulty
- Is able to comprehend a word that has been spelled orally
- Benefits from discussions and small group interactions
- Processes information from lectures
- Usually enjoys making oral presentations
- Often has music or background sounds playing while studying
- May talk constantly just to hear sound
- Is apt to improvise in conversations and presentations
- Often hums or whistles to self while working

## Visual Learner

- Has good comprehension of what has been read
- Benefits from maps, charts, diagrams, etc.
- Absorbs visual cues from a film
- Understands written directions more readily than oral ones
- Prefers to get news from the television or newspaper rather than the radio
- Tends to like a quiet study environment
- Generally relies heavily on visual aids when giving an oral presentation
- Needs to see a word written down to comprehend its spelling
- Is able to visualize abstract concepts in order to problem solve
- Generally looks over puzzle pieces, then chooses correct one
- Likes working from a script rather than improvising

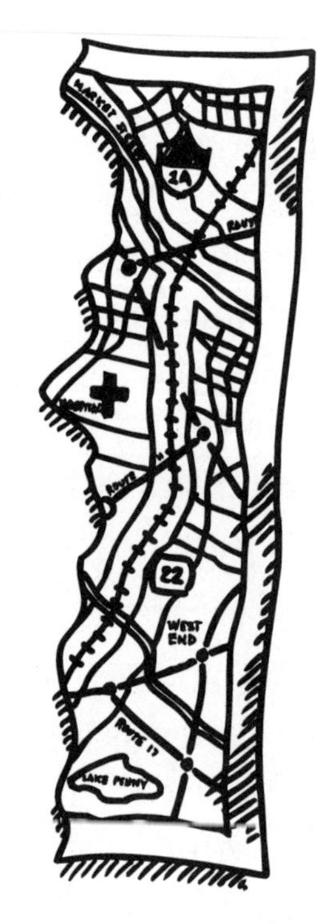

## Tactile Learner

- Learns best by physical acts
- May need to rewrite directions in order to process them
- Cues in on the action in a film
- May exhibit repetitive behaviors, such as foot tapping, finger drumming, or hair twirling, when trying to process information
- Wants to touch, stroke, hold, or move items being used
- Has difficulty sitting still
- May shift and fidget when attempting to give oral presentations
- Benefits most from hands-on activities
- Is often a good problem solver if able to handle concrete objects
- Tends to enjoy mechanical challenges
- Will pick up and try several puzzle pieces before finding the correct one
- Enjoys unusual study positions, such as curling up under tables, wedging into corners, sitting on boxes, etc.

Remember, most students will exhibit a combination of these characteristics. We all learn better if we actually DO something rather than just look at or hear about it. Use these characteristics as guidelines. If you realize a large group of your students learn best through the auditory mode, then adjust your plans accordingly. By varying the presentation style of lessons and activities, you will be able to cover all the bases.

## GENERAL SPELLING STRATEGIES

There are several techniques that can help every child become a better speller. Teach your class these strategies, and guide particular students to techniques that will assist them the most.

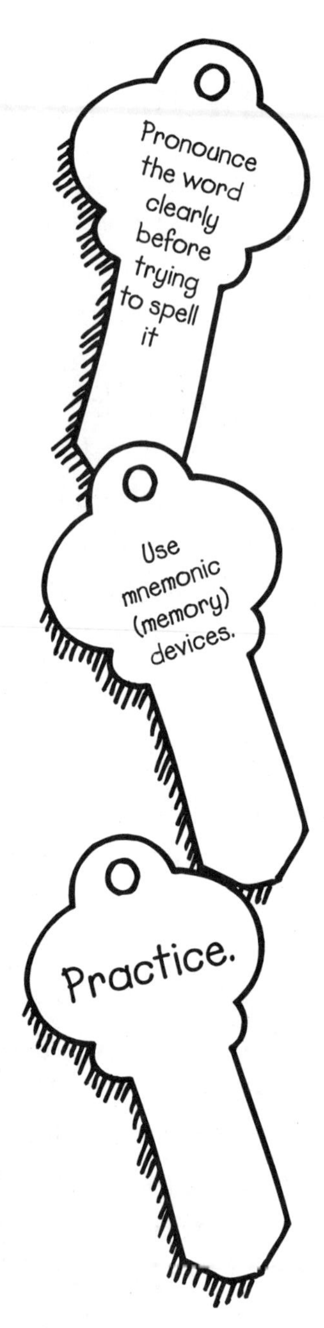


1. **Pronounce the word clearly before trying to spell it.** Some children will need to say the word aloud each time. Other students will get in the habit of saying the word several times in their mind before writing it.

2. **Use mnemonic (memory) devices.** A few mnemonic devices appear in lessons throughout this book. These include old standards, such as *i before e except after c*; mispronouncing a word so that a silent letter is not missed, as in *no TICE able*; and thinking of little stories to help remember a difficult spelling, such as *mnemonic: begins* with an **m** just like **m**emory.

3. **Learn some simple rules, but don't try to make every word fit a rule.** Children will become frustrated by exceptions if they try to make every word work with a given rule, but it is worthwhile to have them study some of the broad generalities in spelling (see "Topic-Specific Activities").

4. **Increase visual memory—picture the word in your mind.** This is a key to better spelling. Use games and practice to increase students' visual memory.

5. **Remember that the dictionary is your friend.** Students should become comfortable with seeking help from the dictionary. Mastering some of the spelling rules first will give them a starting point for dictionary searches. Set a good example by occasionally checking the dictionary yourself. If a student asks you how to spell a word, a good strategy is to say, "Let's look it up together."

6. **Practice.** There is really no substitute for practice. But it doesn't have to be boring—the techniques used in this book are designed to take the boredom out of spelling drills. It is important not to let students get in the habit of just copying a spelling word, letter by letter, from another source. This does nothing to develop visual memory. Rather, teach students to:

**Study** — look carefully at the word
**Cover** — put a paper over the word or look away
**Think** — visualize the word in your mind
**Write** — try writing the word as you have pictured it in your head
**Check** — look back at the word to check the spelling
**Repeat**— if you misspelled the word, repeat the steps

# THE "TERRIBLE SPELLER"

No comprehensive study has ever proven a direct relationship between intelligence and spelling. In fact, history has revealed that George Washington, Thomas Edison, and Albert Einstein all were terrible spellers. Unfortunately, a poorly spelled written assignment often is viewed as an unintelligent presentation. Reinforce to students that being a "terrible speller" does not reflect their intelligence. Spelling requires practice and knowledge of techniques just as any athletic or artistic endeavor does. Here are some strategies for helping the poor speller.

1. **Reinforce strategies.** Work through each of the strategies explained on the previous pages. Create a cue card for the student by writing the strategies on an index card and laminating it.
2. **Highlight what is being done right.** When grading a spelling test or writing assignment that includes specific spelling words, use a green pen or colored pencil to underline the particular words that were spelled correctly. Praise the effort put into the task.
3. **Keep individual graphs.** Place achievement graphs in the "PLUS" section of the student's logbook (page 20). Develop a bar graph formula. Use one color to indicate the number of words the student spelled correctly on the pre-test for the week and, directly next to it, use another color to indicate the number of words correctly spelled on the post-test. The student will be able to see that practice does pay off.
4. **Form an Improvement Club.** Create a series of increasingly more significant awards for levels of improvement. The awards don't have to be fancy. At this age, many students enjoy a coupon that states they may eat lunch with the teacher in the classroom. Another popular coupon is one that allows students to stay inside with a friend and play games instead of going outside during a lunch period. Additional computer time is also a favorite with middle schoolers, as stickers, stamps, and candy treats may continue to be.

5. **Play visual memory games.** Employ some of the following activities to help students develop their visual memory.

- Have the student work with "*Simon*" or other similar electronic toys that produce a series of lights and sounds. The child must repeat the sequence, from memory, in order for the game to continue.

- Place 5–10 objects on a tray. Let the child study the objects. Cover the tray. Have the student list all the items that he or she can remember. Or let the student study the objects. Then, without letting the student see, remove one of the items from the tray. The child must name the missing object. For either game, gradually increase the number of objects.

- Have the student work with punch-out letters when a certain word is troublesome. If the word has a silent letter, such as the **t** in *listen,* cut that letter out of sandpaper or another material with texture. Have the student manipulate the letters and physically form the word. The student should then trace each letter with a finger to reinforce their order.

## THE "SUPER SPELLER"

If a student in your class is a supremely talented speller, you may be concerned about keeping him or her challenged. Here are some strategies you can use to keep this student engaged.

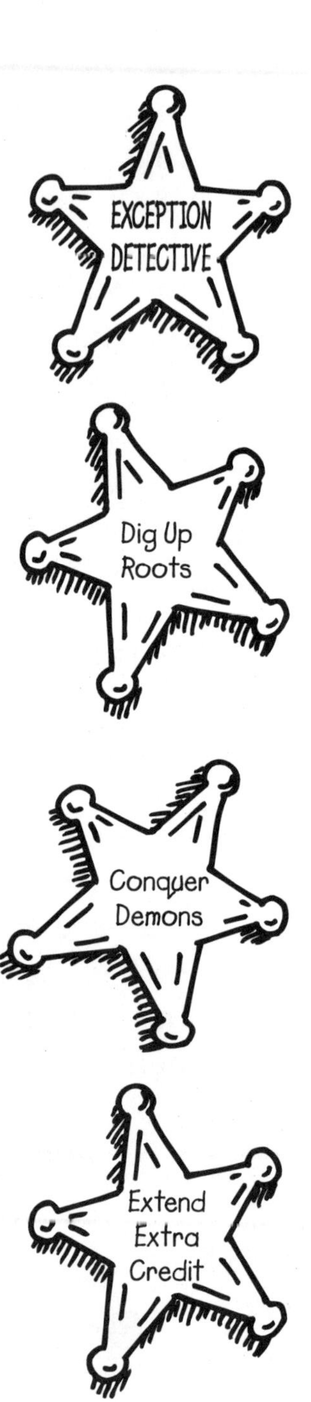


1. **Assign some Exception Detection.** Give the student the task of searching for words that are the exception to a particular spelling rule.

   **For example,** if you are teaching *i before e except after c, or when sounded like a as in neighbor or weigh,* the student might produce a list that includes *ancient, foreign, either, height, seize, weird, efficient, forfeit,* and so on.

2. **Have the student dig up roots.** Give the super speller a root and its meaning. Then have him or her find as many words as possible that contain that root.

3. **Help the student conquer the demons.** Each week let the student choose 20 spelling demons from the list in this book (see p. 125). The student should participate in whatever activities the class is doing, but use the customized list. Test the student for mastery of these words.

4. **Extend extra credit.** Allow the student to develop worksheets of activities such as word searches, cryptoquizzes, and anagrams that utilize the week's spelling words. Place these worksheets in an area where other students may solve them for extra credit. DO NOT use these worksheets as assignments for the other students in order to avoid resentment.

5. **Encourage logbook additions.** In the "PLUS" section of the logbook (see p. 20), the student may work on lists of words in the following categories: *words with more than five vowels, words with the most consonants in succession, words that keep a foreign flavor (buffet, moustache, streusel), longest words, words* that contain ***x*** *or* ***z****, etc.*

6. **Assign the student to come up with a challenge spelling list.** Let the student create a list of 20 interesting words by choosing from a variety of assignments in this book.

7. **Play Bowl-a-Word.** In this bowling game, the student's "pins" are groups of letters. To score a "strike," the student must discover a 9- or 10-letter word. To score a "spare," he or she must rearrange the letters of the large word to form two smaller words—the word can't simply be split into two parts—with no letters left over.

**Examples:**

| | | |
|---|---|---|
| crocodile | cried | cool |
| underwater | return | wade |
| impossible | limbs | poise |
| parakeets | speak | rate |
| necessary | scary | seen |

Have the super speller find as many words as possible that will fit into the game format.

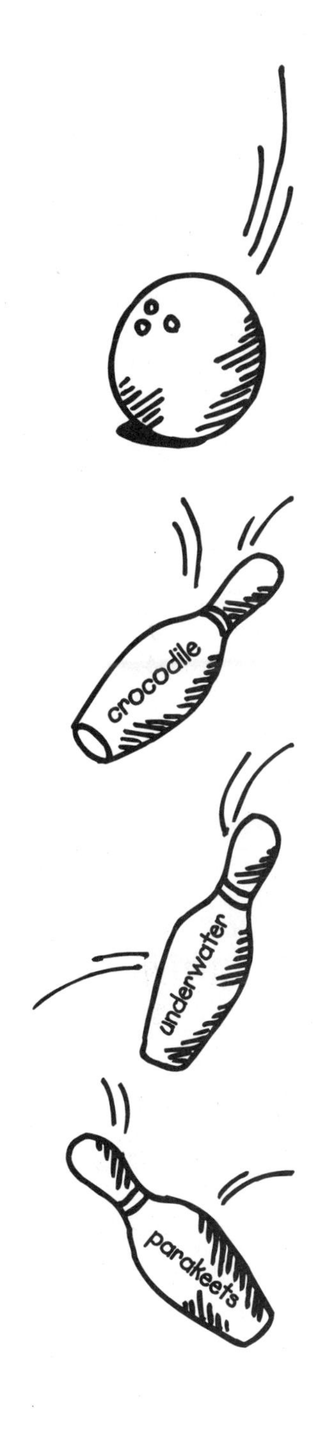

## ADAPTING FOR SPECIAL NEEDS

Most school districts now integrate special needs students into the regular classroom. Certain adjustments need to be made when this is the case.

Often the special needs student has a difficult time focusing during whole class instruction. Be sure that you are physically close to the student when presenting a key concept. Check frequently to see if the child is paying attention. When the class begins individual practice of the concept, be sure to check immediately for understanding on the part of the student. If a spelling rule is presented, write it on a note card and tape it to the student's desk for reference.

It is not unusual for special needs students to lack the visual memory required to learn spelling. Help develop that skill by using some of the games discussed in this book and encourage these students to develop the habit of using spelling aids. "Quick Word" style books, electronic spellers, computer spell-check programs, and dictionaries may all prove helpful.

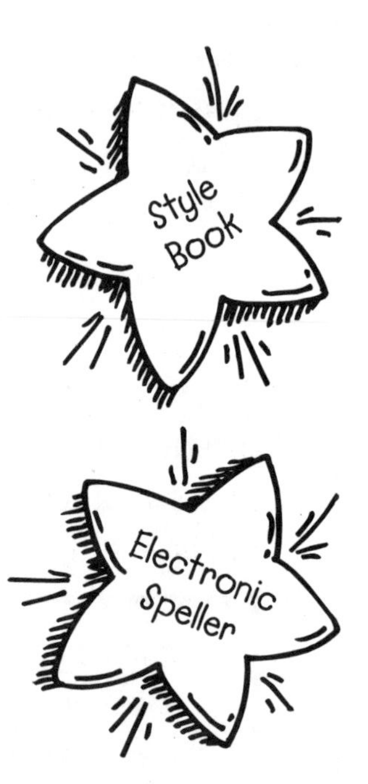

Here are a few more strategies to try to adapt spelling lessons for the special needs child:

- Use mnemonic devices to aid in spelling difficult words. Learning these words will require repetition and practice. General spelling rules will also require plenty of practice.
- Attempt to identify the student's strongest learning mode (see p. 7). Select practice activities that highlight this particular style.
- Reduce the number of words on the child's spelling list.
- Review basic phonics, with plenty of repetition.
- Print all spelling words; cursive can be too confusing for some students.
- Spend time reviewing word patterns (*sight, night, bright, fright,* etc.).
- Don't single out the child. Supervise practice by working with a small group that includes him or her. Small groups can be formed with other children who can use extra practice.
- Help the student utilize the "***study***, ***cover***, ***think***, ***write***, ***check***, ***repeat***" practice technique (see p. 11).
- As with all students, be sure to highlight what the student does correctly. Put special stars or stickers by words that have been spelled correctly on tests or other written assignments.
- Design spelling assignments to test recognition rather than recall. Write each spelling word once correctly and once incorrectly (for example, *mission* or *mishun*). Let the student circle the proper spelling.
- If the student's motor skills make it very difficult to write, allow the child to spell the words orally to you or to type them on the computer.
- Be patient and flexible. As you work with these techniques, you may discover that they help other students in the class as well.

# CLASSROOM MANAGEMENT

## STUDENT CHOICES

If spelling is to be approached energetically by students, the teacher's first step is to be enthusiastic; enthusiasm tends to be contagious. Be bold in your planning. At first glance, some of the activities presented here might appear too elementary for older students. However, I have discovered that students soon become absorbed in the projects.

To help overcome any student reluctance, give the activities catchy titles, such as "Today's Technique" or "Challenge of the Week." Also let students choose the method of practice they'd like to follow. At the beginning of the class, create two columns on a sign-up sheet or on the chalkboard. Entitle one column "Know It," the other "Brave It." Under the first column, print a traditional spelling-practice method to be used for the week, for example, "Write each word five times," "Use every word in a sentence," "Write three paragraphs using all the spelling words," or the like. Under "Brave It," simply place a question mark. Students place their initials under the heading of their choice. They must abide by their decision and may not switch after hearing the "Brave It" option. Once all the students have made their decision, explain one of the projects presented in this book as the "Brave It" activity. All the students who signed up for this option will participate in the project. Students who put their initials under "Know It" will practice using the method listed there.

Menus are another way to place the decision-making process in the hands of the students. Once your class is familiar with several of the methods or activities, you may list them in menu form. Allow the students to pick one of these methods for spelling practice.

# THE SPELLING CENTER

Making use of a classroom spelling center is a very helpful management technique. Load a center with various manipulatives, games, and activities to help the students practice spelling. Then use the center as a source of enrichment or as the focus of weekly spelling lessons.

To outfit your center, scour garage and yard sales for old games that contain letter tiles, cubes, or cards. Wooden puzzle letters or magnetic letters, designed for use on a refrigerator, are also wonderful additions. Keep the various letters in plastic tubs or zipper-style bags. The children may then use them to practice spelling words. Also have on hand a folder loaded with word puzzles that students may attempt during free time.

If you choose to use the center as the means for presenting the weekly lesson, you will need to develop a clear and concise format. Be sure that all necessary supplies are available at the center, or that their location is clearly indicated. Write out precise instructions for whatever project the students will be developing, then go over them orally with the entire class. Be sure to set clear guidelines concerning when students may work at, or obtain supplies from, the spelling center.

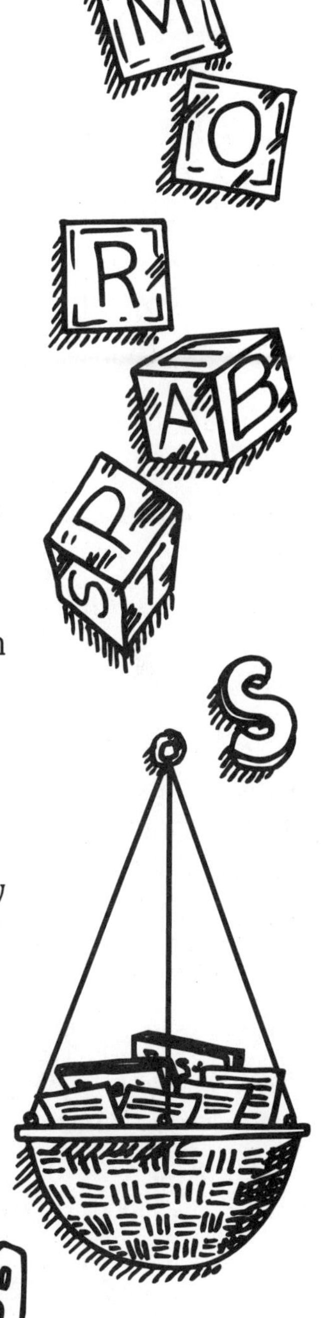

Make certain that the center is appealing and accessible. A simple center to establish is a table in a corner with a piece of poster board or foam board or a small bulletin board just above it for posting instructions. If you don't have a table or the space, try a wide variety of storage options that are available at low prices. Large plastic tubs, stacks of plastic drawers, stacked baskets on wheels, and even hanging baskets can all be used as the basis for a spelling center. Instructions can be written on a piece of poster board and placed in an accessible location.

## LOGBOOKS

Spelling logbooks are wonderful management tools that help students become more responsible for their own learning. For each logbook you'll need a one-inch binder and at least 30 pages of notebook paper. Allow the children to decorate and personalize their binders with permanent markers and stickers. The logbooks should be kept in an accessible location in the classroom.

Logbooks should be divided into three sections. To make dividers, children may use commercially made dividers with tabs, or they may staple small squares of colored paper to the edges of notebook pages. Section 1 should be labeled "Weekly Lists," section 2 "Spelling Rules," and section 3 "PLUS."

PLUS is an acronym that stands for Personalized Learning for Understanding Spelling. In this section, students may develop and include their own individual helps and hints to further their abilities. Here students should begin a list of their own spelling demons—words that may not be particularly tough for other students to spell but that are the most difficult for themselves. Students should also include favorite mnemonic devices for quick reference, as well as achievement graphs. If a child repeatedly misspells a particular word in writing assignments, this word should also be added to this area of the log. Super Spellers (see p. 14) should use this portion of the logbook for their enrichment challenges. And if there is a special vocabulary word from another subject that you want the children to be able to spell, have them add it to the PLUS section as well.

The section marked "Weekly Lists" is for exactly that. Here students should write down the list of spelling words they are currently studying; adding to these lists should become a routine part of your weekly spelling lessons. Be sure to have students head each list with the date or "Week #__" for easy reference. Show the class how to write the words in columns so that at least two or three lists can be written on each page. Encourage the students to write each list of words in alphabetical order. This will assist them in locating a word at a later date.

When studying spelling rules, have the students write each rule in the section marked "Spelling Rules." Include a few sample words for each rule. If desired you may even want to add some of the rule exceptions. After each spelling rule, have the students add a "See Week #___" note to cross-reference the rule and the list of words being studied.

It is very important to have logbook use become a habit. The very first day that a list of words is introduced it should be added to the log. Strongly stress to the class that once a word has been added to their logbooks, they are responsible for being able to spell that word. They may look the word up in their logs, but they may not ask the teacher how to spell the word. Whenever a writing assignment is given, be sure to remind students to use their logbooks for spelling assistance. If you keep a master logbook as well, you will give students the opportunity to see that you value spelling and have available a ready reference for students who have been absent.

# DEVELOPING SPELLING LISTS

Many school districts that support a whole language curriculum do not provide their teachers with formal spelling materials—and if they do, they generally stop providing such materials after the primary grades. If you must create your own spelling lists, here are some possible sources:

- Reading vocabulary words—pull them from basal readers, novels, or other selections currently being read

- Words being misspelled in the students' writing assignments—record and tally them, then create a list of words causing the most trouble
- Vocabulary lists from science, social studies, or even math—integrate with other subjects
- Lists you develop comprised of words that pertain to a given weekly theme (see How to Teach Vocabulary Without Going Crazy [Monday Morning Books] for a wide variety of lists)

- Grammatical-form lists you create that consist of all adjectives, all adverbs, conjunctions, or prepositions
- Current events—the names of people, places, and things currently in the news

- Children's choice lists—let students contribute words they are interested in learning how to spell
- How to Teach Spelling Without Going Crazy —this book provides enough words for an entire school term by presenting spelling rules, prefixes and suffixes, homophones, and spelling demons and commonly misspelled words (see the Contents page for locations)

## WEEKLY PLANS AND ASSESSMENT

There are many ways of incorporating spelling into a language arts curriculum—no particular way is better than another. It is important, however, to find a system that is both comfortable for the teacher and beneficial to the students. Try several different methods until you find the one that works best for you and your class. In the following options, "practice activity" refers to one of the projects listed in this book.

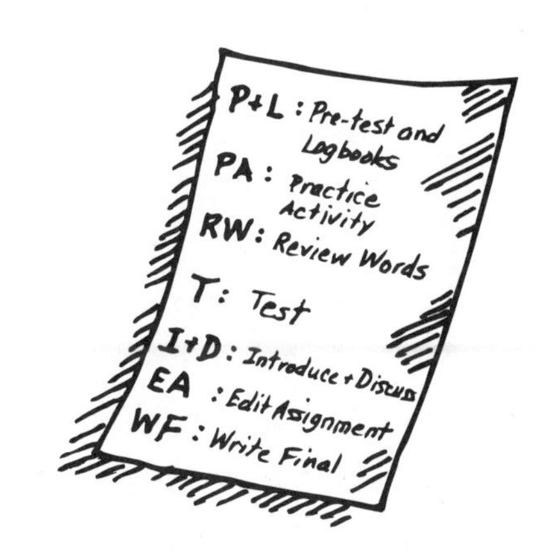


**Option I:**

M—Pre-test and enter the words into logbooks
T—Do practice activity
TH—Review words by using spelling center or discussing practice activity
F—Test

**Option II:**

M—Introduce and discuss list; log words
W—Do practice activity
F—Test

**Option III:**

M—Pre-test and log words
T—Do practice activity
TH—Test
F—Do second practice activity with words missed on test

**Option IV:**

M—Introduce and discuss list; log words
T—Do practice activity
W—Apply work in a written assignment that includes all spelling words
TH—Edit assignment; check for spelling
F—Write final copy of assignment

Formal assessment of spelling words is not a sacred necessity. Many times students do well on the tests and then never spell the words correctly again. However, most teachers are comfortable using some form of spelling assessment. Here are some suggested methods for evaluation:

- **Traditional**—students number papers, words are given orally, students write each spelling word on their paper
- **Recognition**—students are given a worksheet that lists three spellings for each word; they are to circle the correct spelling (this method works very well for special needs students)
- **Unscramble**—students are given a worksheet that contains each spelling word in scrambled form; they are to unscramble and correctly write each word
- **Pronunciation key**—students are provided with the written pronunciation of the word and are asked to write the correct spelling, for example:
  fēnd ___fiend___ trôf ___trough___
  klām ___claim___
- **Sentences**—students are given a worksheet of fill-in-the-blank-style sentences; they write the correct spelling word in each blank (students look at each sentence, the teacher reads aloud three choices of spelling words to be placed in the sentence, students then write the correct word in the blank)
- **Application**—students are given a writing assignment in which all spelling words are required to be included

Sometimes you may want to adjust your assessment technique depending on the difficulty of the words. Other times you may want to change the methods to provide some variety. Be sure to pick and choose the methods that work best for you.

## ANALYZING ERRORS

Part of helping students learn to spell is figuring out where they make their mistakes. Sometimes it takes some fancy detective work to get to the bottom of a misspelling. Following are some common student mistakes that will help you analyze errors.

**Mispronunciation.** Is the child pronouncing the word correctly? I remember puzzling over "badensoot" from a youngster for the longest time. Finally, I gave up and asked the child. She replied, "That's what I wear in the swimming pool, my badensoot," which of course was "bathing suit." Make sure that <u>you</u> pronounce words correctly, too. Many adults say "pitcher" rather than "picture" and "<u>ek</u> cetera" instead of "<u>et</u> cetera." Many newscasters and politicians mispronounce the word "nuclear" as "new-cue-ler." As you introduce words to your students, pronounce them slowly and distinctly. Listen as children are speaking. Gently correct any mispronunciation that may lead to misspelling.

**Following a pattern.** The English language is loaded with inconsistencies; there seem to be more exceptions than rules. Children often misspell words because they are following a pattern or rule that they learned. A student who writes "nere" instead of "near" probably has a firm understanding that a silent e makes the initial vowel long. If a child has learned to spell "bite" and "kite," it may seem perfectly reasonable to believe that "nite," "brite," and "fite" are correct spellings. The fact that these words follow the -ight pattern is an inconsistency that must be learned.

**Using phonetics alone.** Students making this type of mistake have a firm knowledge of each letter and the sound it makes. Their spellings include all the sounds represented in the word, but they fail to include all of the necessary letters. "Tunl" is a phonetic spelling of "tunnel." "Kloz" may be the student's attempt at spelling "clothes." Using phonetics is an early transitional stage for some spellers; sometimes, older elementary students get stuck there. Activities to promote visual memory and significant review will help these students move toward mastery.

**Letter reversals.** As students improve their visual memory of words, they often use all the correct letters but transpose two of them. Some typical reversals are:

| | | |
|---|---|---|
| siad for said | muose for mouse | agian for again |
| gril for girl | thier for their | tow for two |

**Omission.** Silent letters and double consonants are usually the culprits in this type of error. Don't assume that children will automatically remember to place silent letters in their words. Be sure to point silent letters out and reinforce their position. Rules for doubling consonants must be gradually introduced and reviewed. Common examples of this type of error are:

| | | |
|---|---|---|
| lisen for listen | ofen for often | biger for bigger |
| kiten for kitten | peple for people | strech for stretch |

**Addition.** Once children become confident spellers, their love of letters grows. After learning consonant digraphs or silent consonant combinations, they may get carried away, adding extra letters with joyful abandon. Here are some common addition errors:

| | | |
|---|---|---|
| bangk for bank | whitch for witch | macker for maker |
| cadge for cage | beatch for beach | whith for with |

**Regional dialects.** These errors are similar to those caused by mispronunciation. Be sensitive to speech patterns, dialects, and accents in your area. Typical errors of this type are:

| | | |
|---|---|---|
| idear for idea | git for get | pahk for park |
| crik for creek | walkin for walking | ax for ask |
| warsh for wash | foller for follow | |

**Lack of practice and usage.** Students must continually be given the opportunity to write and use the words that they have studied. Although weekly lists and tests play an important role in spelling, they should not be the only way students practice and learn. The following pages give some suggestions for developing significant review methods to help students attain mastery.

In all cases of errors, a big red circle or check mark does nothing to aid students' spelling abilities. Take some time to point out what students are doing well. For example, if they have used all the correct letters, this is an opportunity for praise. Understanding that they simply reversed the vowels will guide them towards correct spelling. Reassure students that learning how to spell takes a long time. The more they read, write, and work with words, the better spellers they will become.

## SIGNIFICANT REVIEW

A common complaint among teachers is that students study and achieve 100% on spelling tests and then spell the very same words incorrectly shortly after the test. To counter this, determine if students have ample opportunity to use their spelling words in addition to during the weekly test. Constant and significant review is necessary to help achieve mastery. The following are a few techniques you can use to promote review.

EAGLE
marsh
leech
singer
BRICK
carpet

- When having students play any of the spelling games in this book, include review words from previous lists as part of the activity.
- Always include one to five previously studied words on each spelling test, without announcing them ahead of time. This will encourage students to learn about spelling, rather than just memorize words. Making students accountable for all spelling words helps them take responsibility for developing their own spelling abilities.
- Give random rewards or bonus points when students correctly spell spelling words in their writing assignments.
- Don't treat spelling as an isolated subject. If new words are introduced in reading, point out when they follow a particular spelling rule or pattern. Have the students add these words to their counterparts in the logbooks. Also encourage the children to point out these types of words as they discover them in their leisure-time reading.
- Design writing assignments that promote the use of words you have been studying.
- Use Spelling Minute Questions. These quick oral quizzes may be used as time-fillers when the children are waiting for the bell or standing in line, or during that pause before morning announcements. The quizzes can also become part of your daily routine, perhaps at the start of each language arts class.

Spelling Minute Quizzes are pointed questions that review concepts and ask students to apply knowledge. Answers may be discussed orally or written into the PLUS section of the students' logbooks. Or students may write their name and answer on a slip of paper and place the slip in a box. One name is drawn out and a prize presented if the answer is correct. Following are some sample Spelling Minute Questions:

button

FIZZ

babies

kitten

1. Remembering the rule of i before e except after c, how do you spell "perceive"?
2. If I tell you the /k/ sound in "squint" is spelled with a q, how would you spell the word?
3. If "accountant" ends with ant, how would you spell "informant"?
4. Remembering the rules for plurals, spell the plural for "perch."
5. List three words that follow the pattern of doubling the final consonant before adding a suffix.

Phonics may also be reviewed using the Minute Question format. The following are sample questions that will help reinforce phonic skills, which in turn should help promote spelling mastery:

1. List three ways to spell the sound /ow/.
2. There are four ways to spell the /k/ sound. Can you name them?
3. Did you know that you could spell the word "fish" ghoti? Why?

(**Answer:** the same letter sounds can be found in enough, women, nation.)

4. How many ways can you spell the sound /shun/?
5. What do c and s have in common?
6. Name a word that uses ph to spell the /f/ sound.

# BULLETIN BOARDS

Bulletin boards can be a wonderful asset to your classroom environment when utilized as a teaching aid. Following you'll find five long-term bulletin board display ideas for which you do the majority of work once, then simply make minor adjustments throughout the year. Each of the following samples produces a permanent background, or template, for display, then gives options for making changes to keep the bulletin board current. Students may be involved in making these bulletin board displays.

## The Camera

Cover the bulletin board with a bright color paper. Use cut-out letters to spell "Picture This" across the top of the display. Cut out a large rectangle of gray paper to form the body of the camera, and place it on the far left side of the board. Add a black circle, topped with a smaller white circle, to form the lens. Add a thin white rectangle to the top of the camera and draw a rectangle to represent the flash. Draw another rectangle and circle for the eyepiece. If you want to make the camera more dimensional, add thin parallelograms to the top and sides. Use a marker to add a few details, such as a shutter button and several knobs or dials. Your background template is now complete.

**Option 1:** Cut out a variety of shapes and sizes of balloons from brightly colored paper. Tie a piece of string to each balloon. (Students may be enlisted to create the balloons.) Write several spelling words on each shape and staple the shapes to the display. (The word "balloon" has a double consonant and a double vowel, so this display is appropriate to use with spelling words containing either of those combinations.)

**Option 2:** In the fall, cut out leaf shapes from red, yellow, orange, and brown paper. Add several words to each leaf and staple the leaves to the background. (The list of words on the display might include "leaf "and "leaves," relating the list to the theme.)

**Option 3:** Cut out a number of brightly colored circles and squares. On the back of each shape, tape a wooden craft stick to create a wide variety of lollipops. Write several spelling words on each lollipop and put them in front of the camera. You could also make displays with the shapes of animals, cars, flowers, snowflakes, stars, insects, boats, hats, birds, rockets, books, t-shirts, musical instruments, sports equipment, or snakes. Whichever shapes you use, try to connect the images with the words in the spelling lists. For example, shapes of candies could display plural words ending in -ies, snakes could present words with a double s, and stars might teach words with the suffixes -ar, -er, and -or.

# Picture This

# The Garden

With a little creativity, this garden design can last the entire year. Think about the seasons and update the display appropriately. Begin by covering the upper half of the bulletin board with light blue paper to represent the sky. Cover the lower half with brown paper for dirt. Be sure that the line where the two colors meet is slightly uneven to indicate the ground. On the right side add a few simple garden tools. Use silver paper to make a spade or a hoe, or cut tool shapes from cardboard and then cover with aluminum foil. To make garden gloves, trace your hands onto bright colored paper and cut out. Add a basket cut from yellow paper. You can achieve a three-dimensional look by stuffing the basket with old tissue paper and using real garden gloves. Your background is now complete.

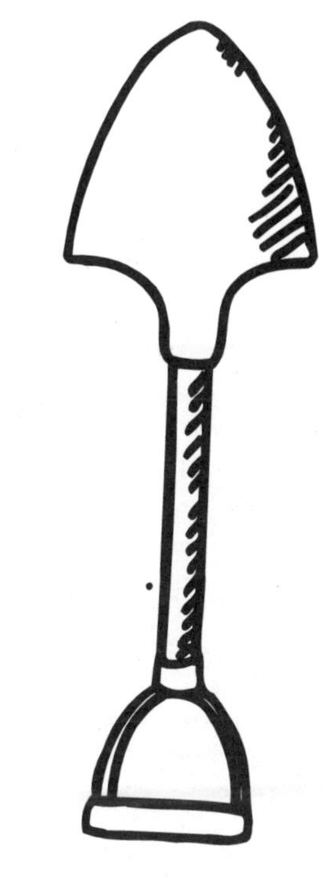

**Option 1:** Add the title "Base Words" across the top of the board. This may be done with cut-out letters or by using a banner format. Cut carrot shapes out of orange paper and write a base word on each. Staple the carrots to the brown paper, being careful to align them with the top edge of the dirt. Cut free-form leaf shapes from green paper and staple to the top of the carrots. Have students form words by adding prefixes and/or suffixes to the base words. They should write these words on the appropriate carrot top. You may wish to start with only one or two carrots and add to the garden as time progresses. This display option is ideal if your class is advancing to the study of roots. You can write root letters on each carrot, then have students find words that are formed from each root and write them on the appropriate leafy top.

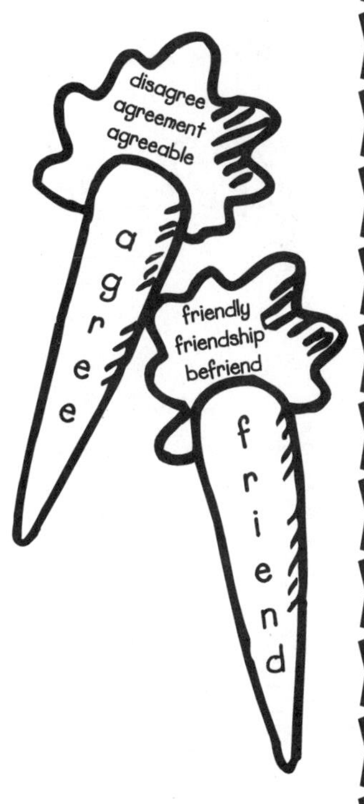

**Option 2:** Using cut-out letters, add the title "Homophones" to the display. Provide students with a wide variety of colored paper. Let each child cut out a flower shape, write a set of homophones on it, and staple it to the board. Once all the flowers are in place, add some green stems and leaves to complete the floral display.

**Option 3:** In the fall, use cut-out letters to create the title "Spelling Harvest." Cut out large orange pumpkins and write several spelling words on each. Attach the pumpkins to the garden. Create vines by twisting and stapling green crepe paper streamers among the pumpkins.

**Option 4:** Once winter has passed, place the title "Spring into Spelling" on the bulletin board. Cut a few small plant shapes out of green paper and place them in the garden. Cut out rabbit shapes from white, gray, and light brown paper. Let each child write his or her spelling words on a rabbit shape. Place the rabbits in the garden. If you are working on doubling consonants in words, make the same display but title the board "Double Trouble."

Base Words
agree
play
able
friend
write
beauty
HOMOPHONES
flower flour
sword soared
break brake
fair fare
paced paste
weigh way
son sun
to too two
pear pare pair
dear deer
pain pane
wear where

# Spelling City

Cover the top third of the bulletin board with blue paper to represent the sky. Place a long strip of black paper along the bottom fourth of the display to indicate a highway. Add white stripes to the road with white correction fluid. Turn the center of the display into a skyline by cutting the silhouette out of one long sheet of paper or by cutting out and placing individual rectangles. Use gray or brown paper to make the buildings. On the far right of the display, place a large white rectangle to act as a billboard. Use cut-out letters to add the title "Spelling City" across the top of the bulletin board. Your background is now complete.

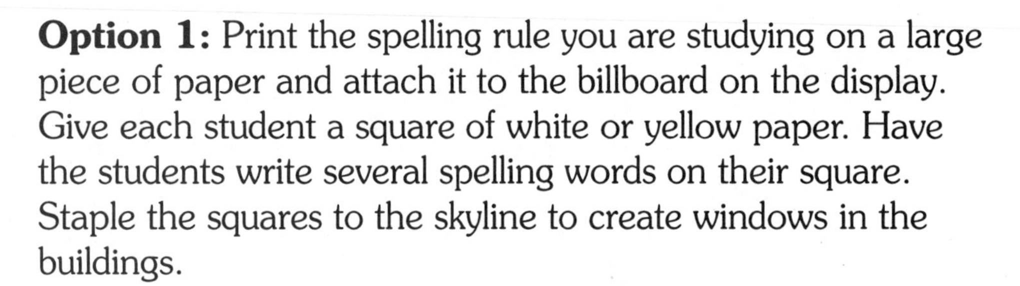

**Option 1:** Print the spelling rule you are studying on a large piece of paper and attach it to the billboard on the display. Give each student a square of white or yellow paper. Have the students write several spelling words on their square. Staple the squares to the skyline to create windows in the buildings.

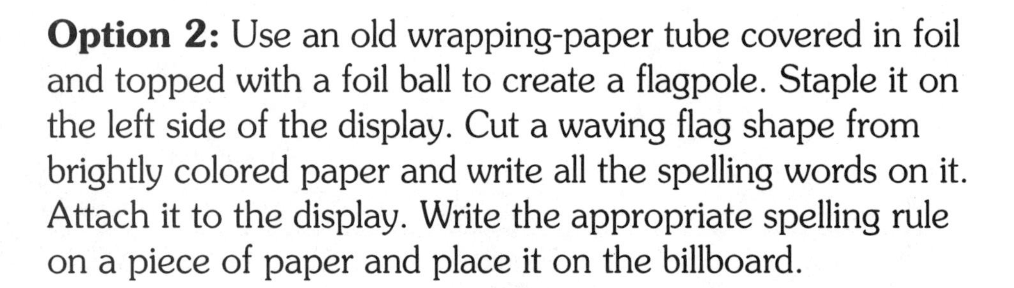

**Option 2:** Use an old wrapping-paper tube covered in foil and topped with a foil ball to create a flagpole. Staple it on the left side of the display. Cut a waving flag shape from brightly colored paper and write all the spelling words on it. Attach it to the display. Write the appropriate spelling rule on a piece of paper and place it on the billboard.

**Option 3:** Let each student cut out a car or truck shape from scrap paper. Have the students write their spelling words on their vehicle. Staple the shapes to the highway in "Spelling City."

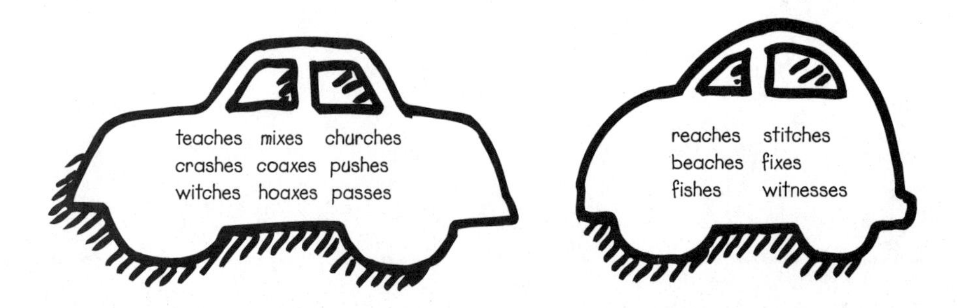

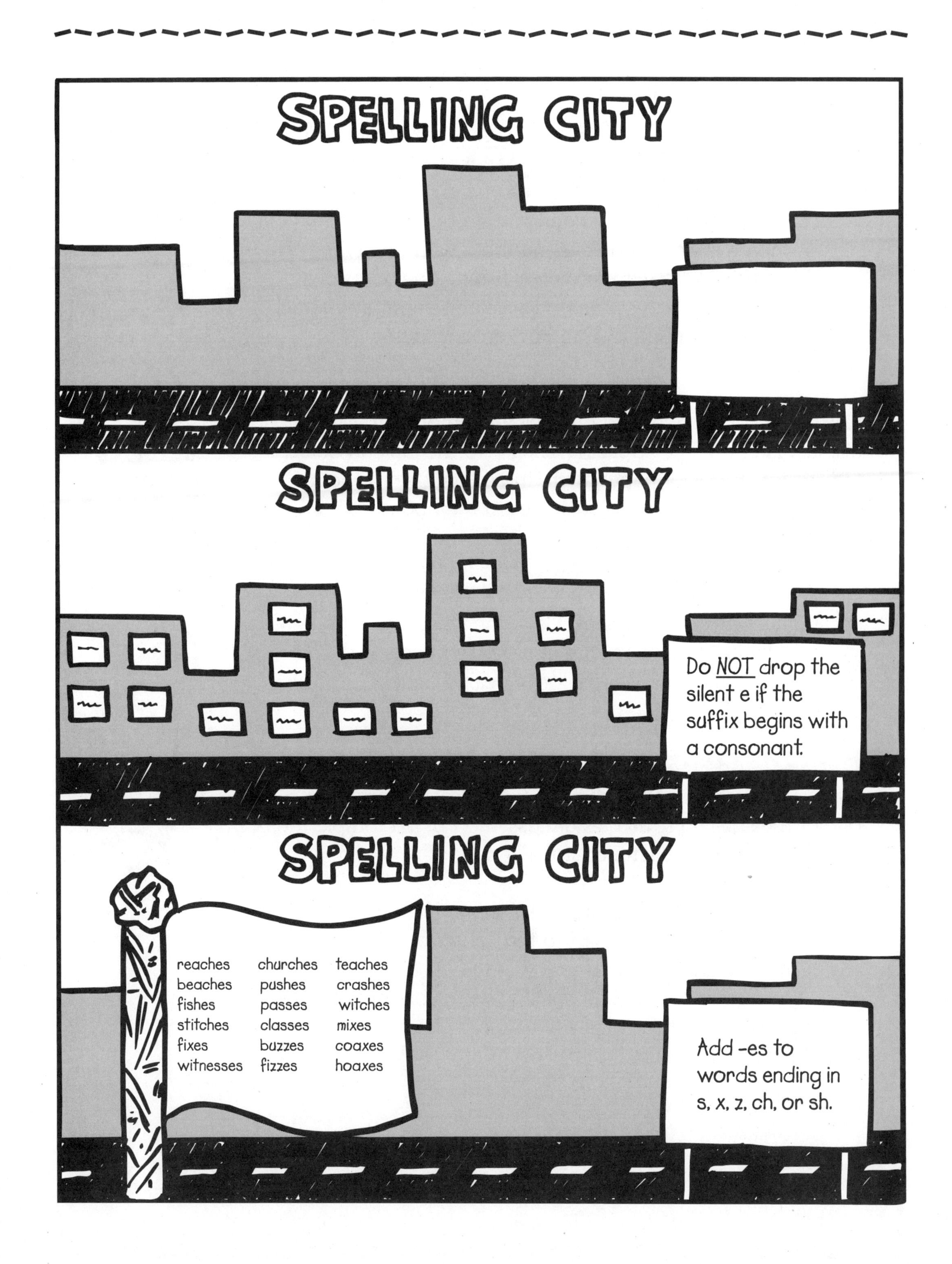
SPELLING CITY
SPELLING CITY
Do NOT drop the silent e if the suffix begins with a consonant.
SPELLING CITY
reaches churches teaches
beaches pushes crashes
fishes passes witches
stitches classes mixes
fixes buzzes coaxes
witnesses fizzes hoaxes
Add -es to words ending in s, x, z, ch, or sh.

# Undersea

Cover the bulletin board with light blue paper. Along the bottom add some brown or yellow paper to represent sand. Cut out a few green leaves of seaweed and place several on the left and a cluster on the right. Create hooks by cutting out cardboard shapes and covering them with foil. Hang the hooks on the display with thread or fishing line. Cut several fish and some shells out of brightly colored paper and attach to the permanent display. Your background is now complete.

**Option 1:** When working on spelling demons, try this display. Add the title "Spelling Snags" to the bulletin board. On several pieces of paper, write the difficult words your class is studying. Hang the words from the hooks.

**Option 2:** Ask students to make fish shapes from colored paper and to decorate them with markers. Assign one spelling word to each student. Have the students write their word on their fish. Add the fish shapes to the display. Use the title "Catch These Words" or "Spelling School" for this option.

**Option 3:** Add the title "Hooked On Spelling" to the display. Create six large fish shapes. On each shape, write one of the spelling strategies discussed on p. 10. Staple the fish shapes to the bulletin board.

**Option 4:** Cut out a treasure chest shape from gray or brown paper. Staple the chest to the center of the board. Give each student a circle of yellow paper to represent gold. Have the students write their spelling words on their gold circle. Staple the circles near the treasure chest and add the title "Words to Treasure" at the top of the display.

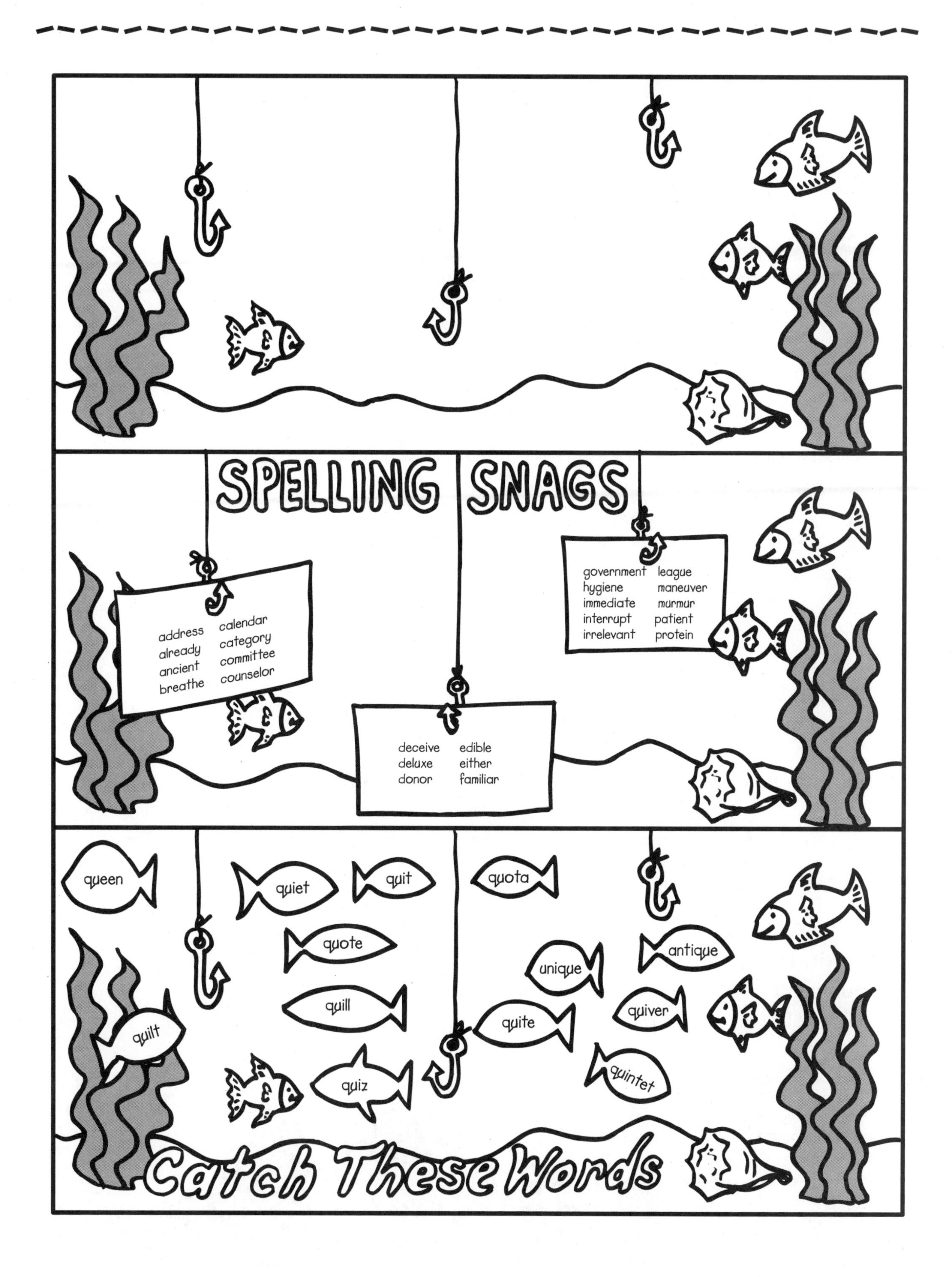
SPELLING SNAGS
address
already
ancient
breathe
calendar
category
committee
counselor
deceive
deluxe
donor
edible
either
familiar
government
hygiene
immediate
interrupt
irrelevant
league
maneuver
murmur
patient
protein
queen
quiet
quit
quota
quote
quill
quilt
quiz
quite
unique
antique
quiver
quintet
Catch These Words

# High-Speed Train

Cover the bulletin board with a bright color paper. About a third of the way up from the bottom, use a ruler to draw a heavy black line. Under the line, draw a series of arches to create a futuristic rail system. Write the title "Put Spelling on a Fast Track" across the top of the display. Using a light color paper, cut out three squares with rounded corners for train cars. Make a rounded triangular shape for the rear of the train. For the engine cut out a quadrilateral that resembles the front of the space shuttle. Add a window to the engine and rear car. Use another color to indicate a circular nose cone on the engine. Add two black or silver wheels under each section of train. Your background template is now complete.

**Option 1:** Using paper cut to the size of the three middle cars, add information to the display. On the first piece write the heading "PREFIX" and include several samples. Write the title "BASE WORD" on the second piece. On the third piece write the heading "SUFFIX" and several examples. Use the papers as a teaching tool when instructing students on word structure.

**Option 2:** Utilize the train cars to show the steps needed to write certain plurals or the past tense of verbs. Write "Change y to i" on the first car and "Add -es or -ed" on the second car. Make a list of these types of words for the third car.

**Option 3:** Write a rule on the first train car. Let students list words that apply to that rule on the other two sections of the train.

Put Spelling On A Fast Track
Put Spelling On A Fast Track
dis- un-
re- ex-
mis- pre-
PREFIX
BASE WORD
-ed -ing
-ful -ment
-tion -est
SUFFIX
Put Spelling On A Fast Track
Change y to i
Add -es or -ed
babies cried
cities tried
countries copied
diaries fired
mysteries

# GENERAL ACTIVITIES

The following activities are designed to be used with almost any spelling list. They accommodate the three different learning styles and strive to eliminate spelling-practice boredom and put some sparkle back into learning to spell.

Many of the activities are also environment friendly. They involve recycled products, create reusable materials, and reduce or eliminate paper use. Our students are slowly sinking in a paper swamp; the number of pieces of paper the middle school child uses each week is staggering. Not surprisingly many schools have begun to limit the amount of money they are willing to spend on paper and copying costs. Even if your school has not put budget restrictions in place, it is a fine idea to look into some painless ways of conserving our resources. While some of the environmentally conscious activities presented here may require a bit more time for preparation, it will be well worth the extra effort if a few trees can be saved. The environment-friendly activities are marked with a tree symbol.

After exploring some of the projects in this book, you may want to look at the lessons you are currently presenting and develop some alternatives that will allow you to reuse, recycle, and reduce.

# Cut-ups

The purpose of this activity is to provide enhanced tactile input and visual memory practice.

**Materials:**
Scissors, old newspapers and magazines, one business-size envelope for each student, list of spelling words

**Activity:**

1. Pass out a newspaper section or magazine to each student and have a large number of additional newspapers and magazines available at a central location. Also give each child an envelope. Have the students place their name on their envelope and decorate it in their free time if they wish.

2. Point out to the class the large letters used in headlines and advertisements. Tell them that these are the letters they will be cutting out and using. They should not attempt to cut out letters from the text of stories because they are much too small.

3. Tell students to search through the papers and magazines to find the letters they need to spell their first spelling word. They should cut out these letters and place them in their envelope. Have them continue this process until they have all the letters they need to spell all of their words.

4. When everyone has finished cutting out letters, provide some practice time. Let one person announce a spelling word. All students should then find the necessary letters and lay them out on their desks. Continue the process until all the spelling words on the list have been spelled out.

5. At the end of practice, collect the envelopes and keep them for future use. When a new spelling list is given to the students, they should first sort through their envelopes and use any letters that have already been cut out. They will then have to search only for the additional letters they need to spell the words on their new list.

# Spelling Symbols

The purpose of this activity is to provide the students with time to practice writing words and to make associations with visual images.

**Materials:**
Dictionaries; drawing paper; pencils, markers, or colored pencils; list of spelling words

**Activity:**

1. Students should first spend some time looking up the definition of each spelling word so that they have a clear idea of its meaning.

2. On drawing paper, show students how to write each spelling word four times so that the words form a box (see below).

3. Within each box, have students create a symbol that appropriately illustrates the meaning of that particular word.

4. Put all the students' work together in a folder or bind them into a booklet so that students can see the way that others have interpreted the meanings of the words.

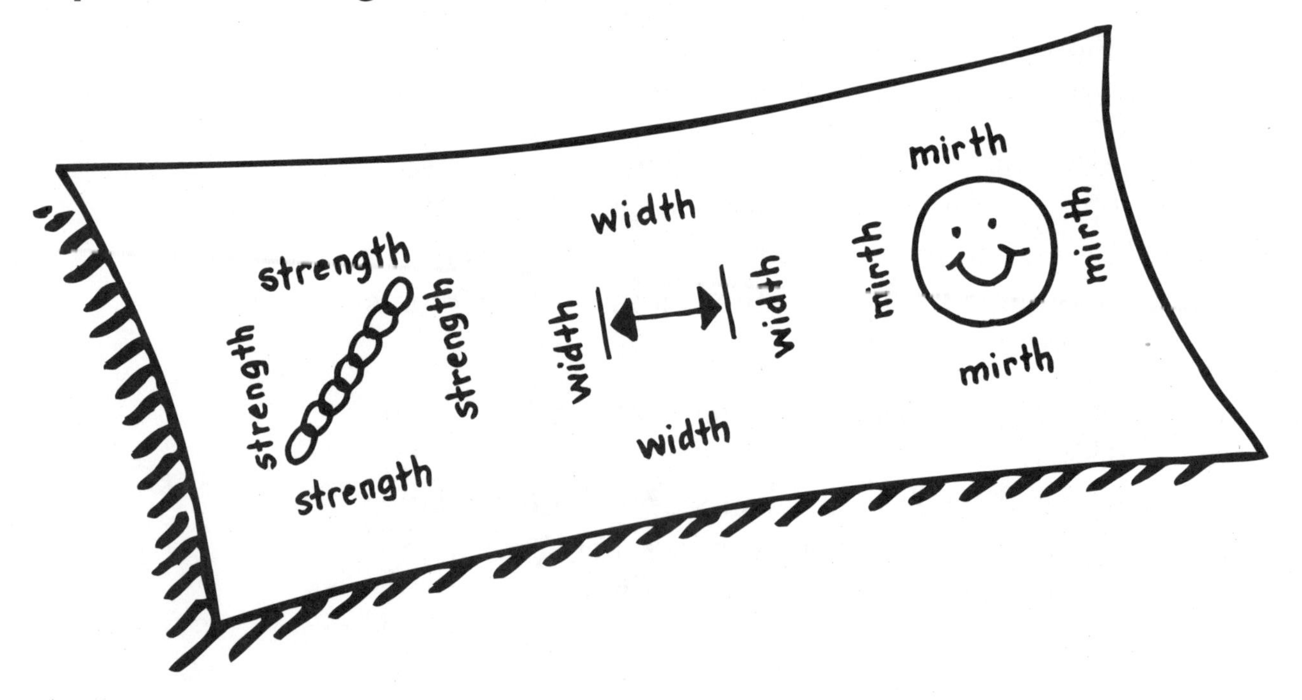

# Word Rainbows

The purpose of this activity is to enable the students to practice writing spelling words and to provide them with an enhanced visual experience.

**Materials:**
Colored pencils, paper, list of spelling words

**Activity:**
1. Write the following letters on the overhead or chalkboard: ROYGBV. Explain to the class that these letters stand for the order in which the colors of a rainbow or spectrum appear (red, orange, yellow, green, blue, violet). The letters are actually a mnemonic device to help remember this sequence when the letters are read as a man's name: ROY G. BiV. The small "i" helps create the last name, but it also stands for indigo, a color on the spectrum found between blue and violet. Indigo is difficult for the human eye to discern, so it is usually included only in scientific endeavors.

2. Have the students pick a sequence of four of the rainbow colors starting with red, orange, or yellow (starting with any of the other colors will not enable them to complete a sequence of four).

3. Tell the students that they are going to write their spelling words in rainbow fashion, using colored pencils and following the sequence they have chosen. For example, if a student chooses the sequence OYGB, he or she should write the spelling word using an orange pencil, then trace over the orange writing with a yellow pencil, then go over the letters using a green pencil, and finally trace over the word with a blue pencil.

4. Students should continue writing all their spelling words in this manner. They may choose a different sequence for each word.

# Craft Stick Puzzles

The purpose of this activity is to provide an enhanced tactile experience and visual memory practice.

**Materials:**

Colored markers, craft sticks (these are available in large, economical quantities), masking tape, list of spelling words, rubber bands

**Activity:**

1. Give each child 10 craft sticks. Have the students lay the sticks side by side on their desks and carefully tape the sticks together using two pieces of masking tape.

2. Have the students turn the sticks over so the tape is on the bottom. The side without the tape is the puzzle surface. Using markers, the students are to carefully write each spelling word on their puzzle. Each letter of the word should be on a different craft stick. Tell the students that it is best to use a different color for every word. Remind them that it will take some planning to be certain that each word will fit.

3. Once the puzzles are complete, students should remove the tape. Have them mix up the sticks and try to put the puzzle back together in the correct order. Allow some time for students to trade puzzles with a friend. Use a rubber band to hold each bundle of sticks together when not in use.

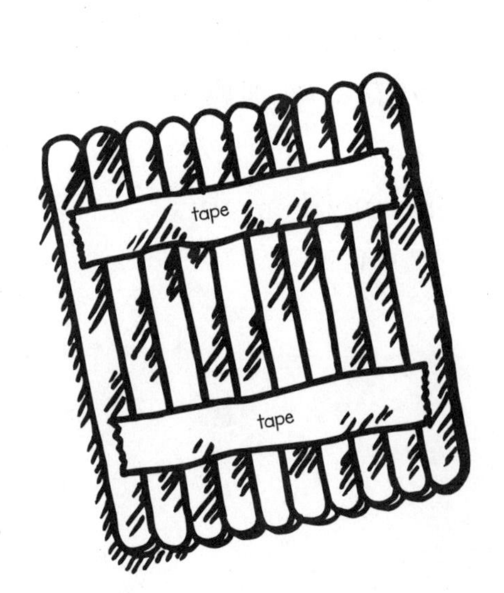

# Shift!

The purpose of this activity is to provide an enhanced tactile experience and to give the students the opportunity to practice writing. (Note: This is a very noisy activity, but a fun one for a gloomy winter day.)

**Materials:**

Pencils, worksheets (see below), tape

**Preparation:**

1. Before class time, create a worksheet that lists each spelling word followed by four numbered lines, for example:

| presence | absence | license | nonsense |
|---|---|---|---|
| 1. _____ | 1. _____ | 1. _____ | 1. _____ |
| 2. _____ | 2. _____ | 2. _____ | 2. _____ |
| 3. _____ | 3. _____ | 3. _____ | 3. _____ |
| 4. _____ | 4. _____ | 4. _____ | 4. _____ |

2. Tape a copy of the worksheet to each desk in the room.

**Activity:**

1. Be sure each student has a pencil. Then have the children look at the worksheet on their desk and choose one spelling word. They should write this word two times below that word.

2. When everyone is ready, call "Shift!" Everyone switches to a new desk and writes a different word two times on the paper on that desk. Keep calling and playing "Shift!" until the paper on every desk is filled. This is a fun way to take the drudgery out of spelling practice.

3. To use this activity as a review unit, create several different worksheets with a variety of words that have been studied over the course of several weeks.

# Balloon Race

The purpose of this activity is provide auditory spelling practice. It's a good one to use as a review.

**Materials:**
Race forms (two are provided on page 50), index cards, dice, list of spelling words, scissors, colored markers

**Preparation:**

1. Make one game kit for every group of four students. The game kit should include:

- one race form, a die
- 20–30 word cards
- and colored markers

2. To create the word cards, take the index cards and cut them into thirds. Write one spelling word on each card. You can include the current spelling words as well as words from previous lessons or words that have been giving the students some trouble. You may want some of the children to participate in preparing the word cards since it will provide extra practice. You can also customize the deck of cards that specific groups use. For example, if you have special needs children in your class, you can give their group simplified words. Super spellers can be given a more challenging deck. Each group may have a different deck of cards and the decks can be rotated among groups for additional game play. Add at least two bonus cards to each deck. Bonus cards should read: "Wind gusts, color two squares. Take another turn."

3. Copy the race forms so that you have enough to give one to each group of four.

**Activity:**

1. Divide the class into groups of four. Give a kit to each group.

2. Explain how the game is played and let the children begin. To play:

> **a.** Each player chooses one of the numbered balloons on the race form. Have the students put their initials in their balloon.
> **b.** The deck is shuffled and all the word cards are placed face down where everyone can reach them.
> **c.** Player 1 rolls the die. The number on the die becomes the value of the word that is drawn.
> **d.** Player 2 draws a word card. He or she reads the word to Player 1, who spells the word. If the word is spelled correctly, Player 1 colors in the number of squares on the race form next to his or her balloon that corresponds to the die roll. If Player 1 does not spell the word correctly, his or her turn ends. In either case, the word card should be returned to the bottom of the pile.
> **e.** Player 2 now rolls the die. Player 3 draws a card and reads the word for Player 2 to spell. Play continues in this manner until one player colors in all the boxes next to his or her balloon, including the one marked "winner."
> **f.** If a bonus card is drawn during play, the player who is about to spell the word receives the two bonus squares mentioned on the card and takes another turn. The bonus card is placed on the bottom of the deck and a new word card is drawn and read for the player to spell.

**Note:** Each race form can be used twice if students use light-colored markers, such as orange or yellow, for the first race. The second race can be run by coloring over the boxes using darker colors, such as red, green, or blue.

BALLOON RACE

1 | | | | | | | | | | | | | | | | | winner

2 | | | | | | | | | | | | | | | | | winner

3 | | | | | | | | | | | | | | | | | winner

4 | | | | | | | | | | | | | | | | | winner

BALLOON RACE

1 | | | | | | | | | | | | | | | | | winner

2 | | | | | | | | | | | | | | | | | winner

3 | | | | | | | | | | | | | | | | | winner

4 | | | | | | | | | | | | | | | | | winner

# Chain Link Sentences

The purpose of this activity is to have students write spelling sentences, in a manner which forces them to think creatively and use complex sentence forms.

**Materials:**
Notebook paper, pencils or pens, list of spelling words

**Activity:**
1. Students are to write a sentence for each spelling word. The challenge is that the last word of a sentence must become the first word of the next sentence.

> **Example:**
> We saw skyscrapers way off in the **distance**.
> **Distance** may be measured in kilometers or **miles**.
> **Miles** away, in an agricultural area, a colt was being **born**.
> **Born** in poverty, the industrialist worked hard to build his financial **empire**.
> **Empire** building is a dream for many business executives.

2. Students should underline each of their spelling words.
3. Be sure to give students plenty of time to complete the assignment; this is a tough endeavor.

# Spelling Scribbles

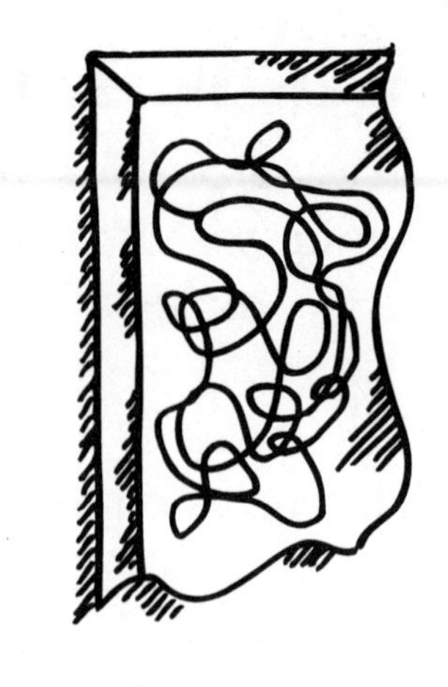

The purpose of this activity is to have the children practice writing words and obtain enhanced visual experience.

**Materials:**
Drawing paper; colored pencils, markers, or crayons; list of spelling words

**Activity:**

1. Give each child a sheet of drawing paper.

2. Ask the class if they remember making "scribble" designs when they were very young. Draw a quick sample on the board.

3. Tell the students that they are to draw a scribble design on their paper. Be sure to have them leave wide open spaces in the drawing.

4. Tell students that they are to choose a spelling word and write it at least four times in one of the spaces on the drawing. They are to continue to do this until all the spelling words have been written at least four times into the design. If the students use a different colored pencil or marker for each word, artistic products will result.

# Cross-Country Race

The purpose of this activity is to provide auditory spelling practice.

**Materials:**

Large map, cardboard backing slightly larger than the map (you can obtain a large piece by flattening a large cardboard box, then cutting open and unfolding one hinged side), three different colored pushpins, one die, three large index cards, red marker, tape, list of spelling words for the teacher

**Preparation:**

1. Tape the map to the piece of cardboard (foam display board can also be used). If you have bulletin board space available, you may post the map there.

2. Use the red marker to create a long, meandering route across the map. At every city along the route, place a red dot. Since this activity can be used over an extended period of time, the longer the route, the better. Be sure to clearly mark the beginning of the route and the final destination.

3. Create three game cards using the index cards. Write the following directions on each card:

- Roll a 1 or a 2—you may get help from teammates
- Roll a 3, 4, or 5—solo spell
- Roll a 6—out of gas

**Activity:**

1. Divide the class into three teams. For explanation purposes here, the teams will be called Green, Blue, and Yellow. Place three pushpins, in coordinating colors, at the start of the route. Give each team a game card for reference.

2. The first player from the Green team rolls the die. If he rolls a 1 or 2, his teammates may help him spell the word that is announced. If he rolls a 3, 4, or 5, he must spell the word by himself. If the player rolls a 6, the team is out of gas. No word is attempted and play moves to the next group.

Announce the spelling word to the first Blue player. If she spells it correctly, advance the blue pin one dot along the route. Play then moves to the next group. But if the Blue team player does not spell the word correctly, say, "You are sightseeing, no advancement." (This is less discouraging than "Wrong, you lose your turn!") Play then moves to the next team.

3. Play continues in this manner until the final destination is reached. This could take several weeks, depending on how much time is allotted. You may wish to use this activity as a review for four or five spelling lists. If you use it for only one list, you will need to repeat some of the words during the course of the game. Whenever possible, make sure that all students have at least one turn each time the cross-country race is taken up.

4. If you like, you can integrate this game with other curriculum areas. For example, you can find out if the social studies class is studying a particular country and use that map for the race. Perhaps Colonial America is the current topic. Students could travel by "horseback" and, instead of running out of gas, they could visit the village blacksmith to have a horseshoe repaired.

# Recipe Riot

The purpose of this activity is to provide practice in writing words.

**Materials:**
Pencils or pens, notebook paper, index cards, list of spelling words, samples of recipes from various sources

**Activity:**
1. Read and show the class several examples of recipes. On the board, show the standard format for writing recipes. Have students note that the ingredients and their amounts are listed first, followed by the procedure. If a recipe indicates how many servings it makes, lists the number of calories in each portion, and includes serving suggestions, point this out.

2. Tell students that they are to create a recipe using their spelling words. Each spelling word needs to be used at least twice in the recipe. (This is easy to accomplish since a word may be written in the ingredient list and then again in the procedure.) Explain that you realize that some of the recipes may sound kind of silly, but that they should follow the standard format.

3. Tell the children that recipes may be created for things other than food. Some possible ideas are recipes for:

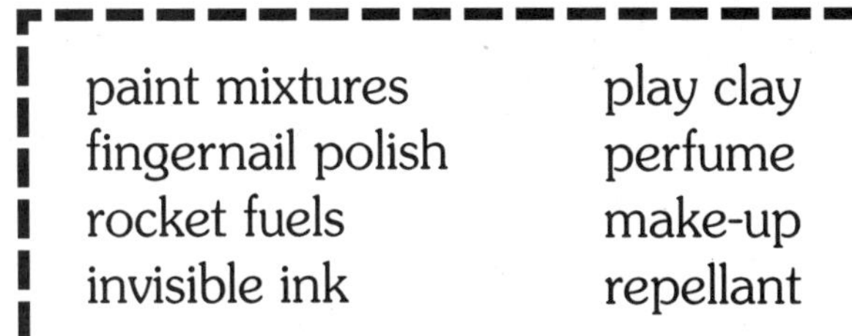

| | |
|---|---|
| paint mixtures | play clay |
| fingernail polish | perfume |
| rocket fuels | make-up |
| invisible ink | repellant |

4. After the students have completed their recipes and edited them, have them rewrite the recipes on index cards. Collect all the cards and keep them in a file box and, if you like, let the children write additional recipes throughout the year. The recipes make fun alternatives to books during reading time.

# Camouflage

The purpose of this activity is to have the students practice writing words and to provide them with an enhanced visual experience.

**Materials:**

Drawing paper; crayons, colored pencils, or markers; list of spelling words

**Activity:**

1. Explain that camouflaging is a means of hiding an object while in plain view. Let students share what they know about camouflage. Bring up the fact that animals often use camouflage to protect themselves. Tell the children that they are going to develop a drawing that will camouflage their spelling words.

2. Give each child a sheet of drawing paper. Tell students that they are to create a drawing that includes their spelling words as part of the picture. The words can be used to shade an area, develop lines, or define shapes.

3. The drawings must include each spelling word written at least five times, and all words must be legible. Tell students that using colors will help with the camouflage illusion. For example, if students fill in a leaf form with spelling words, writing the words with a green crayon or pencil will help camouflage them.

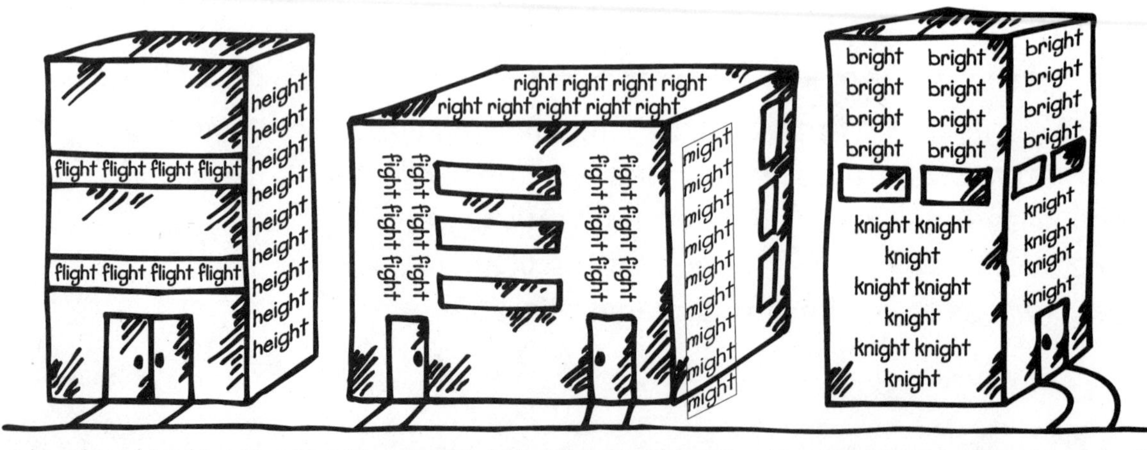

# Soft Spelling

The purpose of this activity is to provide students with a tactile experience and visual memory reinforcement.

**Materials:**
Brown paper grocery bags, scraps of yarn, white glue, scissors, pencils, list of spelling words

**Preparation:**
Cut the bottom off the grocery bags and open each bag up to form a flat surface. Cut these papers in half or thirds, depending on the size background you'd like the students to have for their yarn letters.

**Activity:**

1. Give each child one piece of brown paper. Pass out several lengths of yarn to each student, but do not pass out any glue at this point.

2. Let the children take some time to experiment ways of forming letters with the yarn. Some students may wish to use the yarn to create cursive forms, while others will prefer to use small pieces in order to form block letters.

3. When you feel the students are ready, have them use their pencils to write each spelling word on their brown paper to use as patterns. Remind the children to make fairly large letters since they will be covering their writing with yarn.

4. Pass out the glue. Have students put glue on one letter they have written. Have them add pieces of yarn to the glue to create that letter. Tell the students that trying to put glue on an entire word at one time is too messy, and that they will get frustrated when yarn sticks to the wrong place. Forming one letter at a time will help the project go more smoothly. Students should continue adding glue and yarn to each letter until they have spelled all their words.

# Spell, Rock, and Rap

The purpose of this activity is to provide auditory input and practice writing words.

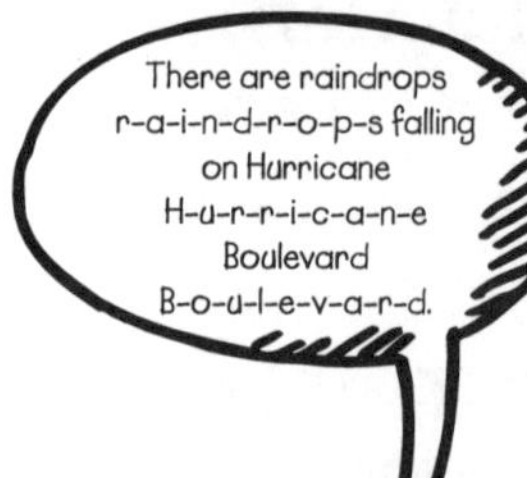


**Materials:**
Tape recorder, blank cassette tape, paper, pencils, list of spelling words

**Activity:**

1. Divide the class into five groups. Assign each group four spelling words from the current list.

2. Tell the students that they are to come up with a rap song that includes their assigned spelling words. Sometime during the song they must spell out each of the words. Give students time to work. If they prefer, you may let students use a cheer format for their presentation.

3. Have each group perform their rap song or cheer for the class while you record it on tape.

4. After all the songs have been recorded, have students get out paper and pencils. Play the tape. Each time students hear a spelling word, they are to write it down on paper.

**Variation:** Most children love to hear themselves perform solo. To do this, let a student say a spelling word and spell it aloud as you tape. Continue around the room until each student has had a turn. Repeat words as often as needed for all to participate. Play the tape for the class. Have the students write the spelling words on their paper as they are spelled aloud.

# Clay Tablets

The purpose of this activity is to provide tactile input, have the students practice writing words, and integrate spelling with other parts of the curriculum.

**Materials:**
Non-hardening clay, toothpicks, waxed paper, plastic bags with zipper-style closings, list of spelling words

**Activity:**
1. Spend a short time talking about early civilizations that existed before the invention of paper. The Sumerians, Assyrians, Babylonians, and Mesopotamians used clay tablets for writing. One form of this writing was called "cuneiform," in which a combination of wedge-shaped characters was imprinted into clay. Library books or talking to the social studies teacher will provide you with information about cuneiform or other ancient forms of writing and about early cultures that you can share with the class.

2. Give each child a square of waxed paper, a cube of clay, and several toothpicks. Tell the class to use the waxed paper as their work surface.

3. Have students work with their clay until they are able to shape it into a small, flat slab.

4. Students should use the toothpicks to write their spelling words, five times each, in the clay. Have them write the first word five times, smooth out the clay with their fingers, write the second word five times, and so on until all the words have been written.

5. When the activity is finished, students should form their clay into balls and store the balls in the plastic bags for future use.

# Significant Searches

The purpose of this activity is to have the students practice writing words and reinforce their visual recognition.

**Materials:**

Graph paper, pencils, list of spelling words

**Activity:**

1. Give each student a piece of graph paper.

2. Tell the class that they are going to create their own special word search puzzles.

3. The students should start by filling in the blank squares with their spelling words. The words may be written vertically, horizontally, or diagonally. It is suggested that you do not allow students to put words in backwards, since that may be confusing and will hinder visual memory of the order of the letters in each word.

4. Each spelling word must appear two times in a puzzle and the two words must be joined in some way (see the sample below).

5. When all the spelling words have been written in the puzzle, the students should fill up the other squares with random letters.

6. Have the students exchange puzzles and solve them. A ring should be placed around both instances of each spelling word as they are found.

7. Place copies of the unsolved puzzles in a learning center for students to solve at other times.

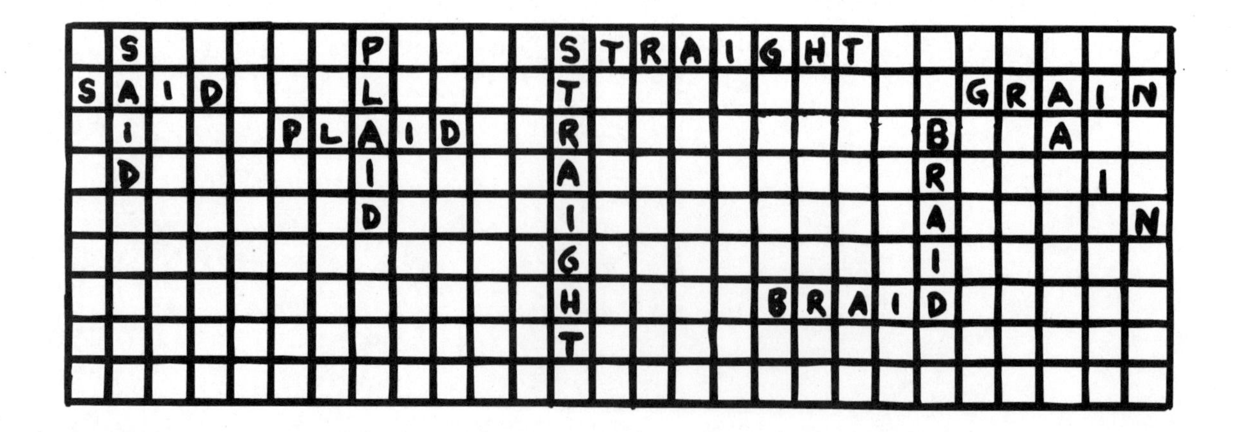

# Skywriting

The purpose of this activity is to provide enhanced tactile input and to have the students practice writing words.

**Materials:**

Easy Project: blue paper, white chalk, crayons, list of spelling words
Messy Project: drawing paper, white crayons, blue tempera paint, paintbrushes, newspaper, water, list of spelling words

**Activity:**

1. Ask the class if anyone has ever seen skywriting. Explain to the students that skywriting is a method of writing in the sky with an airplane. A trail of smoke, produced by mixing a special preparation with the plane's fuel, traces the letters. People on the ground can see the gigantic white letters against the blue sky for many miles. Some advertisers use skywriting to promote their products.

2. To do the Easy Project: Give each child a sheet of blue paper and a piece of chalk. Tell the students to use the chalk to write their spelling words three times each somewhere on the blue paper. Have them add a crayon drawing of an airplane to their projects.

3. To do the Messy Project: Give each child a sheet of drawing paper and a white crayon. Have the children use the crayons to write their spelling words three times each on the paper. They will need to press firmly so that each letter is formed with a solid crayon line. Encourage students to add an airplane to their pictures.

Cover a work area with old newspaper. Thin the tempera paint slightly with water. Let students brush over their entire papers with the blue paint. The crayoned words will magically appear in white as the background becomes blue.

# Spelling Spirals

The purpose of this activity is to have the children practice writing words and to provide them with an enhanced tactile and visual experience. It often inspires students to write their spelling words over and over again.

**Materials:**

Books and magazines with illustrations of various types of spirals, drawing paper, pencils or pens, list of spelling words

**Activity:**

1. Show students a wide variety of spirals. These may be shells, screws, coils, springs, ramps, or staircases.

2. Give a sheet of drawing paper to each child. Have the students begin in the center of the paper and create a spiral with just their spelling words. They may write the words in any order, but each word must appear at least six times in the spiral. Remind the class that the words must be legible.

# Extra! Extra! Write All About It!

The purpose of this activity is to have the students practice writing words in context.

**Materials:**

Newspapers, paper, pencils, list of spelling words, blank newsprint (optional), scissors (optional), glue (optional)

**Activity:**

1. Show examples of several newspaper stories. Read some of the stories to the students.

2. Discuss how the headlines attempt to sum up the story and grab the attention of the reader.

3. Remind students that a good newspaper story will tell who, what, where, when, why, and how. Identify these points in several of the examples you discussed.

4. Tell the students that they are to write a newspaper story that contains all of their spelling words. They may write about an actual occurrence or they may create an imaginary story that depicts an exciting event. Each student's story should include a headline.

**Optional:** Develop a class newspaper. Have the students cut and paste their stories into newspaper format. Use blank newsprint, folded the way newspapers are folded. Let students fill in empty spaces with illustrations that correlate to their stories.

# Spelling Soccer

The purpose of this activity is to have the students practice auditory spelling.

**Materials:**
Soccer field illustration (see "Preparation" for various formats), coin or sticky note and scissors, die, list of spelling words for the teacher

**Preparation:**
1. To draw a soccer field on an overhead transparency: Use a green marker to draw the field and to make appropriate hatchmarks and field markings. Use a red marker to indicate one goal and the hatchmark directly in front of it. Use a blue marker to identify the opposite goal and the hatchmark directly in front of it. (See the sample below.) Use a coin to represent the soccer ball.

2. To draw a soccer field on poster board: Draw hatchmarks and field markings on the poster with colored markers. Use paper from a sticky note to cut out a small soccer ball (this will allow you to keep the ball attached to the playing field).

3. To create a soccer field on felt: Use a large rectangle of green felt for the field. Use white fabric paint in squeeze bottles to create the hatchmarks and field markings. Use red and blue fabric paint to identify the two opposing goals. Use a circle of white felt for the soccer ball (the ball should stick to the playing field even if the field is hung from a vertical surface).

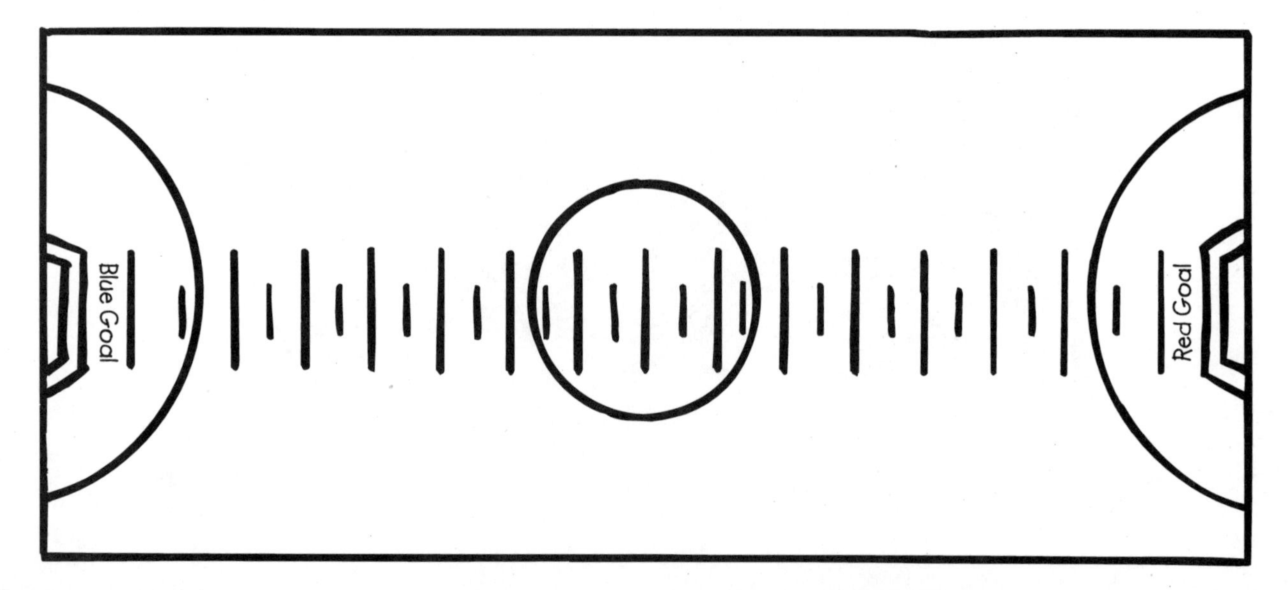

**Activity:**

1. Divide the class into two teams. Here they will be referred to as Blue and Red. The Blue team will play whenever an even number is rolled. The Red team will participate if an odd number is rolled.

2. Place the soccer ball on the center line of the field. Indicate in which direction each team will attempt to move the ball. Roll the die. If a 2, 4, or 6 is rolled, then the Blue team takes possession of the ball. If a 1, 3, or 5 appears, then Red has the ball.

3. Announce a spelling word to a player on the team that has the ball. If the word is spelled correctly, then the ball is moved forward one hatchmark. If the word is not spelled correctly, the ball is not moved. Have play continue in this manner with a player rolling the die after each attempted spelling. The player must attempt to spell the word without any help from team members. Remind the class that you are the referee and may penalize any unruly team member. Shouting out letters or any form of unsportsmanlike conduct should result in a penalty. Consequences may range from the loss of a turn to having the other team move forward one hatchmark toward the goal.

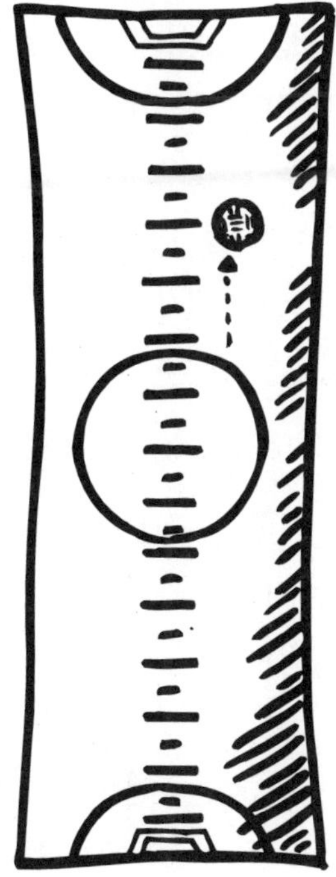


4. When the ball moves to the final hatchmark before a goal, the team in possession of the ball gets a chance to score. But instead of rolling the die, ask the team to spell one final word. Team members may confer during an attempt to score. If the word is spelled correctly, the team scores a point. The ball is returned to the center of the field and the opposing team takes possession of the ball for the next spelling word. If the team does not score, the ball is returned to the center of the field and the game proceeds with the roll of the die.

5. Continue playing the game for a set time limit or for as long as it takes to complete a predetermined number of words.

# Quilt-a-Word

The purpose of this activity is to have the students practice writing words and work with patterns. The activity can be integrated with other curriculum areas.

**Materials:**

Graph paper, colored pencils, magazines or books with color photographs of quilts, list of spelling words

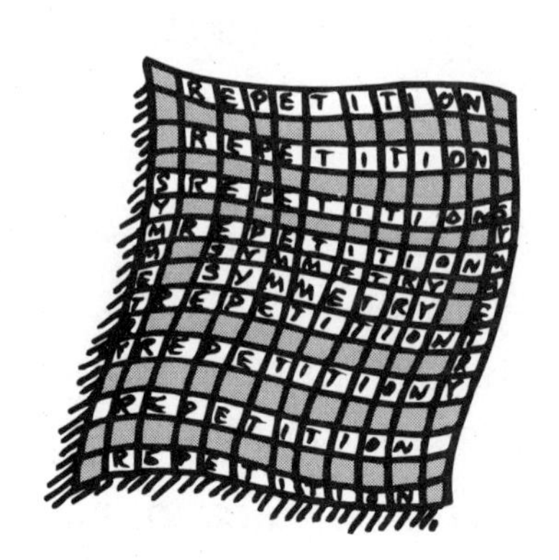

**Activity:**

1. Show the class various photographs of quilts or diagrams of quilt patterns. Ask the students what they think some of the patterns are called and why. Point out that each quilt pattern has a name.

2. Discuss and define the following vocabulary words: pattern, symmetry, and repetition. Point out how each of these words relates to quilts.

3. Give one sheet of graph paper to each student.

4. Tell students they are going to create their very own quilt patterns. They should use the graph paper to develop their patterns by writing spelling words in the boxes, one letter per box. Each word should appear at least three times on the quilt.

5. Remind the students to keep repetition and symmetry in mind as they develop their patterns.

6. After the students have filled the words in the boxes, the blank squares should be colored in with the pencils. The use of color should enhance the quilt pattern.

7. Have students come up with a name for their newly developed quilt pattern.

8. If possible, invite a quilter to come to your class to speak.

# Newspaper Scavenger Hunt

The purpose of this activity is to have the students practice visual recognition and identify word patterns.

**Materials:**

Newspapers; markers, colored pencils or crayons; list of spelling words; scissors (optional); glue (optional); large piece of paper (optional)

**Activity:**

1. Tell students that they are going on a scavenger hunt to find their spelling words. Give each student a page of newspaper that has plenty of text.

2. Explain the word "scan" to the class. Let the students know that they do not need to read every word on the newspaper page. They are to look over the page and try to find their spelling words somewhere in the text. If they find a word, they should circle it with their marker. Have students keep working until all words have been found, or for a certain length of time.

**Optional:** After students have had a chance to search, have them cut out the words they have found and glue them onto a large piece of paper to create a collage of spelling words.

**Variation 1:** Divide the class into groups. Each group should use a designated color marker or crayon. Give a newspaper page to each group. Have the groups spend 7–10 minutes scanning their pages and circling words. Then have each group pass their pages to another group and look again. Groups may not place another circle around a word that a previous group found. Continue for as many exchanges as desired. At the end of the time period, the group with the most circled words wins the scavenger hunt.

**Variation 2:** Reinforce word patterns by allowing students to circle words in the newspaper that have the same pattern as a spelling word.

**Example:**

If the spelling word is "bland," then students may circle words such as land, sand, hand, stand, strand, band, command, island, etc.

# Name That Word

The purpose of this activity is to improve visual memory, auditory input, recall of spelling words, and to provide practice writing words.

**Materials:**
Game grids (see next page), pencils, envelopes, strips of paper, list of spelling words

**Activity:**

1. Divide the class into pairs. Give each pair an envelope, enough strips to write one spelling word on each, and one game grid for each child. Have the children write one spelling word on each strip of paper and place the strips in the envelope. Students should then put away their spelling lists.

2. To play the game:

**a.** Partner A draws a word from the envelope and announces the first letter but does not reveal the word.
**b.** Partner B writes that letter in box 5 and writes her guess of what the correct word is in the "My Guesses" box. If she guesses and spells the word correctly, she scores 5 points and her turn ends.
**c.** If Partner B does not guess and spell the word correctly, Partner A announces the second letter, which Partner B writes in box 4.
**d.** Partner B once again tries to spell the entire word, writing it in the same "My Guesses" box. If she is correct, she scores 4 points and her turn ends. If not, another letter is given, and so on.
**e.** If a student is unable to spell the word correctly by the time box 1 is filled, then no points are given. At the end of each turn, the word is always correctly written in the "Correct Spelling" box by the partner who attempted to guess the word.
**f.** Play alternates between partners until all the words have been spelled. The winner is the partner who scored more points.

# Name That Word

| 5 | 4 | 3 | 2 | 1 | My Guesses | Correct Spelling | Score |
|---|---|---|---|---|---|---|---|
| | | | | | | | |
| | | | | | | | |
| | | | | | | | |
| | | | | | | | |
| | | | | | | | |
| | | | | | | | |
| | | | | | | | |
| | | | | | | | |
| | | | | | | | |

# Map Fun

The purpose of this activity is to provide practice writing words. The activity may be integrated with other parts of the curriculum.

**Materials:**

Markers, colored pencils, or crayons; large sheets of drawing paper; rulers; list of spelling words

**Activity:**

1. Tell the students that they are going to create a map of an imaginary place. List the things that you wish them to include in their maps. Some suggested requirements are:

- title
- landforms
- cities
- compass rose
- map key
- scale of miles
- bodies of water
- roads
- clear labels on all items

2. Tell students that they must use their spelling words to name the features on the map. Each spelling word must be used at least once on the map.

**Examples:**

A mountain range might be named Arrogant Mountains.

A road could be called Defendant Drive.

A location may be named Informant Village.

3. After the maps have been created, give the students a writing assignment. Students should write a paragraph that would provide the reader with a grand tour of the place they have created. In the paragraph, each spelling word must be used at least twice.

# A Maze Thing

The purpose of this activity is to provide practice writing words and to use visual recognition.

**Materials:**
Pencils or pens, colored pencils, mazes (available from a variety of activity books), list of spelling words

**Preparation:**
Make enough copies of a maze for each student to have one. You may wish to provide a variety of patterns so that students have a selection from which to choose.

**Activity:**
1. Give each child a copy of the maze.

2. Tell students to write their spelling words five times each throughout the maze.

3. With a colored pencil, students should then create a path through the maze that will pass through each spelling word at least three times. Students may double-back in the maze but should not cross over barriers.

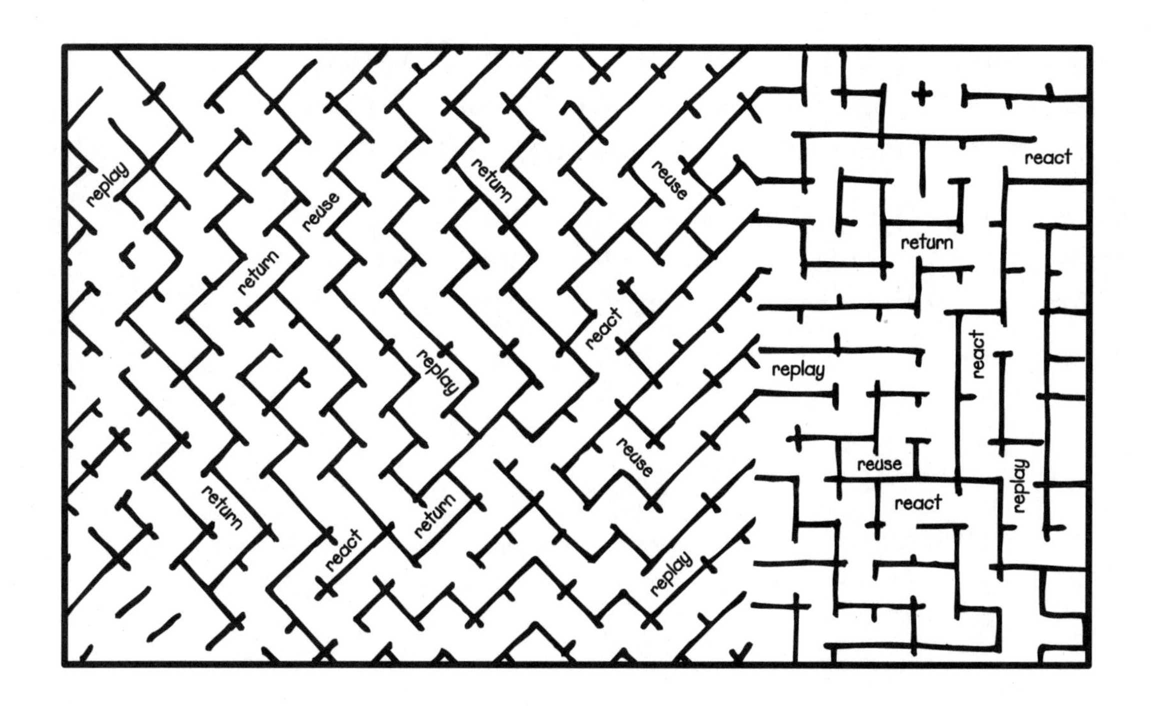

# Spelling Relay Race

The purpose of this activity is to provide auditory input, an enhanced tactile experience, and visual memory practice.

**Materials:**
Chalkboard and chalk or large pages of newsprint and markers, list of spelling words for the teacher

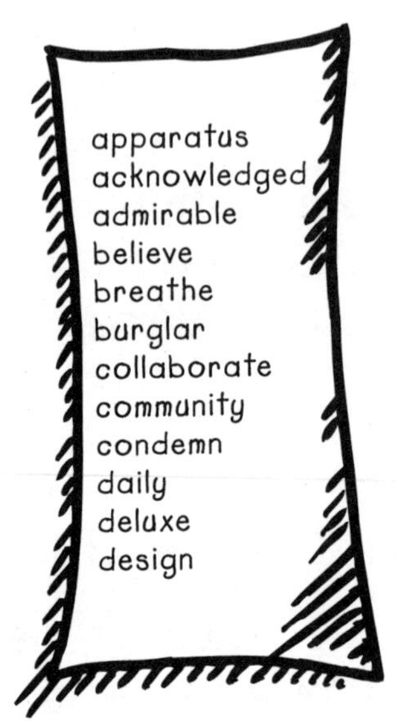


**Activity:**

1. Divide the class into four teams.

2. Each team is given a spot on the chalkboard or a large piece of newsprint. Clearly label each team's location.

3. Establish the order within each team in which members will take turns.

4. Call out a spelling word. The first player on each team goes to the board and writes the first letter of the word. Those players then return to their team and hand off the chalk or marker to the next person. The second set of players then places the second letter, the third set of players the third letter, and so on.

5. The players who place the final letter of the word may make any changes necessary to spell the word correctly.

6. The first team to spell the word correctly earns 2 points. Every other team that spells the word correctly earns 1 point. (This assures that all teams keep trying throughout the round.)

7. Continue play until all spelling words have been completed. The relay is also a great way to practice for a unit review or to reinforce words that the class has been having problems with.

# Spelling Pizza

The purpose of this activity is to provide practice writing words and an enhanced tactile experience.

**Materials:**
Brown grocery bags, red and orange markers, scraps of colored paper, scissors, glue, list of spelling words.

**Preparation:**
Cut off the bottoms of the grocery bags so that you have several large, flat pieces of brown paper. Depending on the size desired, cut three or four large circles from each piece.

**Activity:**

1. Tell the students they are going to make pizzas using their spelling words. Give each child one circle of brown paper.

2. Have the students write their spelling words, three times each, in the center of their brown circle with a red or orange marker. This will give the illusion of "pizza sauce." Encourage the students to leave the edge of the circle free of any writing to represent the crust.

3. Students may now cut out "toppings" from the scraps of paper to add to their pizzas: shapes of pepperoni, sausage, ham, mushrooms, onions, peppers, olives, anchovies, pineapple chunks, or shredded cheese. They will need one topping shape for each spelling word.

4. Have the students write one spelling word on each topping and glue the pieces to their pizza creations.

5. Encourage each student to name his or her special pizza. If desired, allow time for students to come to the front of the class and describe their culinary masterpieces.

# Print It!

The purpose of this activity is to provide tactile enhancement of writing and to focus on the order of letters. The activity works best if located in a learning center that small groups of students can visit as time allows.

**Materials:**
Rubber stamp alphabet set, ink and inkpads in various colors, large sheets of drawing paper, stencils in various letter styles, markers or colored pencils, rulers, list of spelling words

**Preparation:**
Set up a work area. Provide stamps, paper, inks, stencils, markers, and colored pencils.

**Activity:**
1. Since some children may be unfamiliar with the supplies, demonstrate the use of stamps and stencils. Be sure to show the students how to determine if a stamp is right side up. If this is difficult to tell on your stamp set, consider marking a dot or an arrow on each stamp to help enable correct placement. Explain to the class the use of the stencils. Point out that the children may want to draw a light pencil line, using their rulers, to act as a guide for the stencil.

2. Ask the students to create a colorful poster of their spelling words. They may use any combination of the materials provided.

# Simon Says: Write . . .

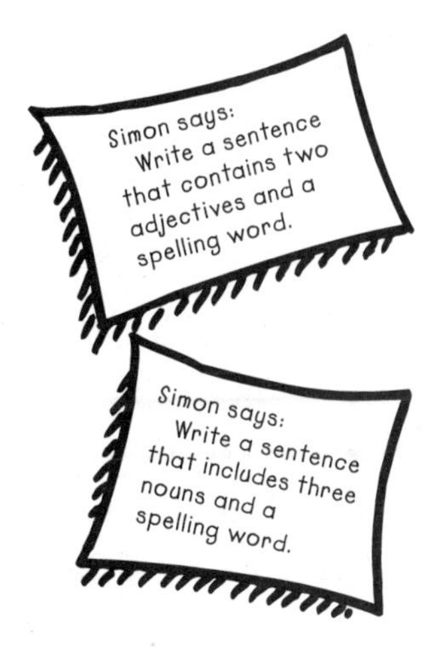


The purpose of this activity is to provide practice writing words in sentence format.

**Materials:**
Index cards, paper and pencils, list of spelling words

**Preparation:**
Before class, prepare the index cards. Write one instruction on each of at least 10 index cards. Each card should begin with the words "Simon says," followed by a specific instruction. Here are some instructions that could be placed on the cards:

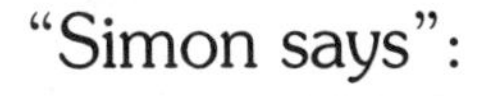

"Simon says":

- Write a sentence using three spelling words.
- Write a sentence in which a spelling word is the FIRST word.
- Write a sentence in which a spelling word is the LAST word.
- Write a sentence using two spelling words.
- Write a sentence that contains your name and a spelling word.
- Write a sentence that contains two adjectives and a spelling word.
- Write a sentence using your best friend's name and a spelling word.
- Write a sentence that contains two adverbs and a spelling word.
- Write a sentence that includes an animal and a spelling word.
- Write a sentence that contains the name of a famous person and a spelling word.
- Write a sentence that includes two verbs and a spelling word.
- Write a sentence that includes three nouns and a spelling word.

- Write a sentence that might be found in the comics and uses a spelling word.
- Write a sentence that might be found in a scary book and uses a spelling word.
- Write a sentence that includes a number and a spelling word.
- Write a sentence that includes a color and a spelling word.
- Write a sentence that might be found in a science book and uses a spelling word.

Instructions may also be geared to correlate with any current curriculum you are studying.

**Activity:**

1. Tell the students that they are going to write 10 spelling sentences, but that they are going to be very specific sentences.

2. Have one student come up and choose an index card. He or she should read the instruction to the class. Students should then write the required type of sentence on their papers, underlining each spelling word. Tell the students that once a spelling word has been used, it may not be used again in another sentence.

3. Continue in this manner until the desired number of sentences have been completed.

4. If you do not wish to run this as a whole class activity, you could list the instructions on the board or overhead as they are read aloud. Students could then work at their own pace to complete the task.

**Variation:** A large number of instruction cards (at least 30) could be placed at the spelling center. Students would go to the center, choose a card, complete the task, return the card, and select another, continuing until at least 10 sentences have been completed. To allow for greater flexibility, students could work in pairs, choosing one card at a time. This would leave a larger variety of cards available for other students.

# Crossword Creations

The purpose of this activity is to provide visual memory review and practice writing words.

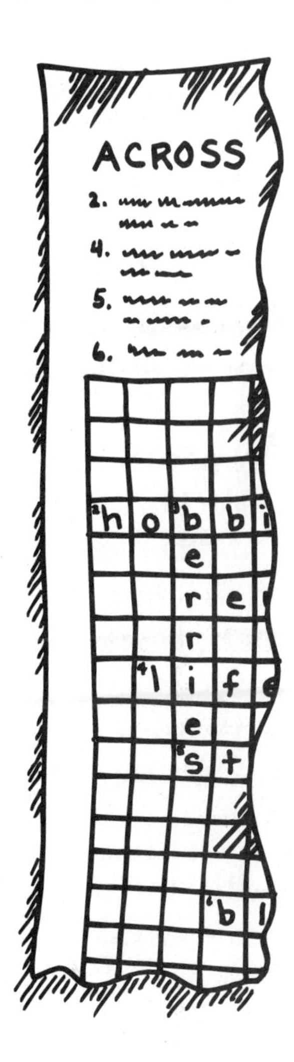


**Materials:**
Graph paper, pencils, samples of crossword puzzles, list of spelling words

**Activity:**

1. Show the class various crossword puzzles. Indicate all the parts to a puzzle. Remind students that the number of each clue, or definition, matches the number of the location where the word is to be written in the puzzle.

2. Have the students write a clue or definition for each of their spelling words next to the appropriate word on their list.

3. Next, have the students mark out an actual puzzle on a sheet of graph paper. A good way to do this is to have them write the clue number in the desired square, then outline the number of squares needed for that word, and do this for each of the words. Point out to the children that if a square is shared by more than one word it must contain only one letter shared by those words. Require students to use all of their spelling words in the puzzle. Once all the spelling words have been placed, the class may add additional words to their Crossword Creations.

4. Any empty squares should be blacked in and all clues should be written at the bottom of the page.

5. Let the students take partners and exchange puzzles. Have them read the word clues and fill in the Crossword Creations with the correct spelling words.

# Fountain of Fonts

The purpose of this activity is to have the students enhance their visual memory and practice writing words.

**Materials:**
Pencils or pens, paper, a wide variety of samples of computer fonts and samples of other print styles, list of spelling words

**Preparation:**
Collect or print out samples of a large variety of computer fonts and other examples of print types. Make enough copies to give one set to each student, or create a folder of samples that students may view.

**Activity:**
1. Take some time to explain to the class the characteristics of the various fonts and how the different letter styles are formed.

2. Tell the students that they are going to try to duplicate some of the fonts. They may use ideas from the samples or make up their own styles.

3. Have students write each spelling word in three different font styles.

**Variation:** If it's possible for all students to have access to computers, they can keyboard their words using the available fonts.

# Silent Spelling

The purpose of this activity is to provide the students with an enhanced tactile experience and practice auditory spelling.

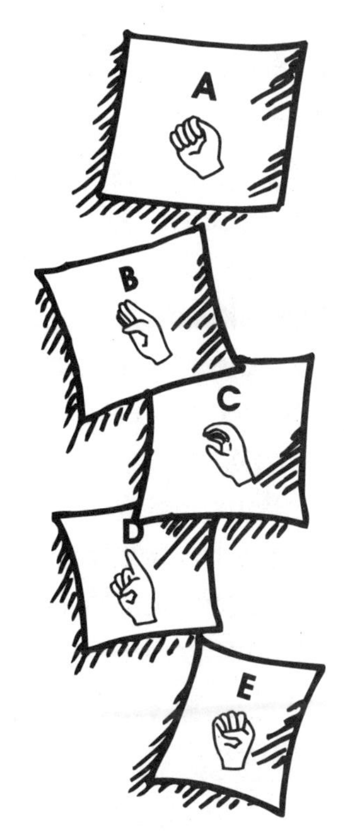


**Materials:**

Chart showing the sign language alphabet (check with the library for a source), list of spelling words

**Preparation:**

1. Make enough copies of the sign language alphabet to give one to each child. If possible, laminate the copies for continued use.

2. Post at least one copy of the chart in the classroom.

**Activity:**

1. Give each child a copy of the chart. Work with the children over several different short sessions to teach them the sign language alphabet. When signing, it is important to keep your elbow still and not bounce your hand excessively. It may help the children if you tell them to imagine that their elbows are set in concrete.

2. Once the children are familiar with the alphabet, let them work in pairs. One child should sign each spelling word while the other interprets by saying each letter aloud as it is signed. After one word has been spelled, the partners should reverse roles. If you introduce this activity at the beginning of the year, students' abilities will increase as the year goes by.

**Note:** Children are fascinated by and enjoy using sign language and are able to learn the alphabet very quickly. Often their interest leads them to go beyond the alphabet and learn words and phrases as well. If it is possible, arrange to have a person fluent in sign language visit your classroom.

# Fancy Stuff

The purpose of this activity is to have the children practice writing words. The activity can integrate with other areas of the curriculum.

**Materials:**
Samples of illustrated manuscripts; drawing paper; colored pencils, pens, crayons, or markers; list of spelling words

**Activity:**
1. Spend some time showing the class examples of illustrated manuscripts. Point out the intricate border designs and the fanciful style on the initial letters.

2. Tell students that they are to design a fancy-style initial letter and design for each of their spelling words. (Depending on the length of the list you are using, you may want to reduce the number of designs required or allow students to combine words that have the same first letter.)

3. Require that each spelling word be written at least four times in the design.

# Comic Relief

The purpose of this activity is to provide an enhanced tactile experience and to have the students practice writing words in context.

**Materials:**

A good number of newspaper comic strips, pencils or pens, paper (you can use scraps or the backs of old worksheets), scissors, glue, list of spelling words, several large pieces of plain newsprint (optional)

**Preparation:**

1. Ahead of time, ask students and staff members to bring in the Sunday comics or some daily comic strips; the activity will be easier and more creative if a good variety of strips is available. You will need at least five to seven individual strips for each child.

2. Ask several students to cut apart the comics pages so that you have individual strips to pass out to the class.

**Activity:**

1. Hand out five to seven comics to each student or put all the strips at a center where students may pick their own.

2. Point out to the class the dialogue balloons in the strips. Explain the difference between words being spoken (shown in a balloon that ends in a point near the character who is speaking) and words being thought (shown in a balloon above the character's head, with smaller, empty balloons below it that decrease in size). Some comic strips omit balloons and simply draw a line from the words to the character speaking. If you have comics in which the dialogue or punchline is written under the drawing, be sure to point out and discuss this format.

3. Tell the students that they are going to modify their comic strips by changing the words in the dialogue balloons. They are to use their spelling words to create new dialogue or a punchline for each strip. They must write as many strips as necessary to use all their words. Assure students that they don't have to make the strips funny. The sentences they write should simply make sense and correspond to the drawings in the strips.

4. Have the students write their new sentences on a piece of paper first. These should be checked for content and spelling. When the sentences are appropriate for the context of the pictures, let the students move on to the next step.

5. Using small scraps of paper, students should create new balloons to fit over the original ones. Students should write their new sentences on the balloons and glue them to the strips.

6. The reworded comics may be glued to large pieces of newsprint for a newspaper comics section.

# Capture

The purpose of this activity is to provide auditory spelling practice.

**Materials:**

Index cards, Capture grids (see the following page), list of spelling words, spelling logbooks, pencils, scissors

**Preparation:**

Make game kits for the class. You will need one game kit for every two students. Each game kit should include:

- 1 Capture grid
- 10 index cards that have been cut into thirds, resulting in 30 small cards

**Activity:**

1. Divide the class into pairs. Give each pair a game kit. Have the students write one spelling word on each of the small cards. If necessary have the students choose additional words from their spelling logbooks to make a total of 30 cards.

2. Have the children play Capture. The object of the game is to connect the dots on the grid to form the most squares.

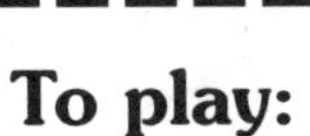

**To play:**

Place the spelling word cards face down between the players. Player Red draws a card and reads the word aloud to Player Blue. Player Blue must attempt to spell the word. If correct, Blue may connect any two dots on the grid. Connections may be made horizontally or vertically, but never diagonally. If Blue does not spell the word correctly, his or her turn ends. Whether spelled correctly or not, the word card is returned to the bottom of the pile. Blue now draws a card and reads the word to Red. Player Red attempts to spell the word, and so on. Play continues, alternating between the two players.

Each time a square is completed by connecting two dots, that player should place his or her initials in the square and then draw an additional line segment. Players should continue to capture squares and draw additional lines until no other squares can be completed. At the end of the game, the player with the most captured squares is the winner.

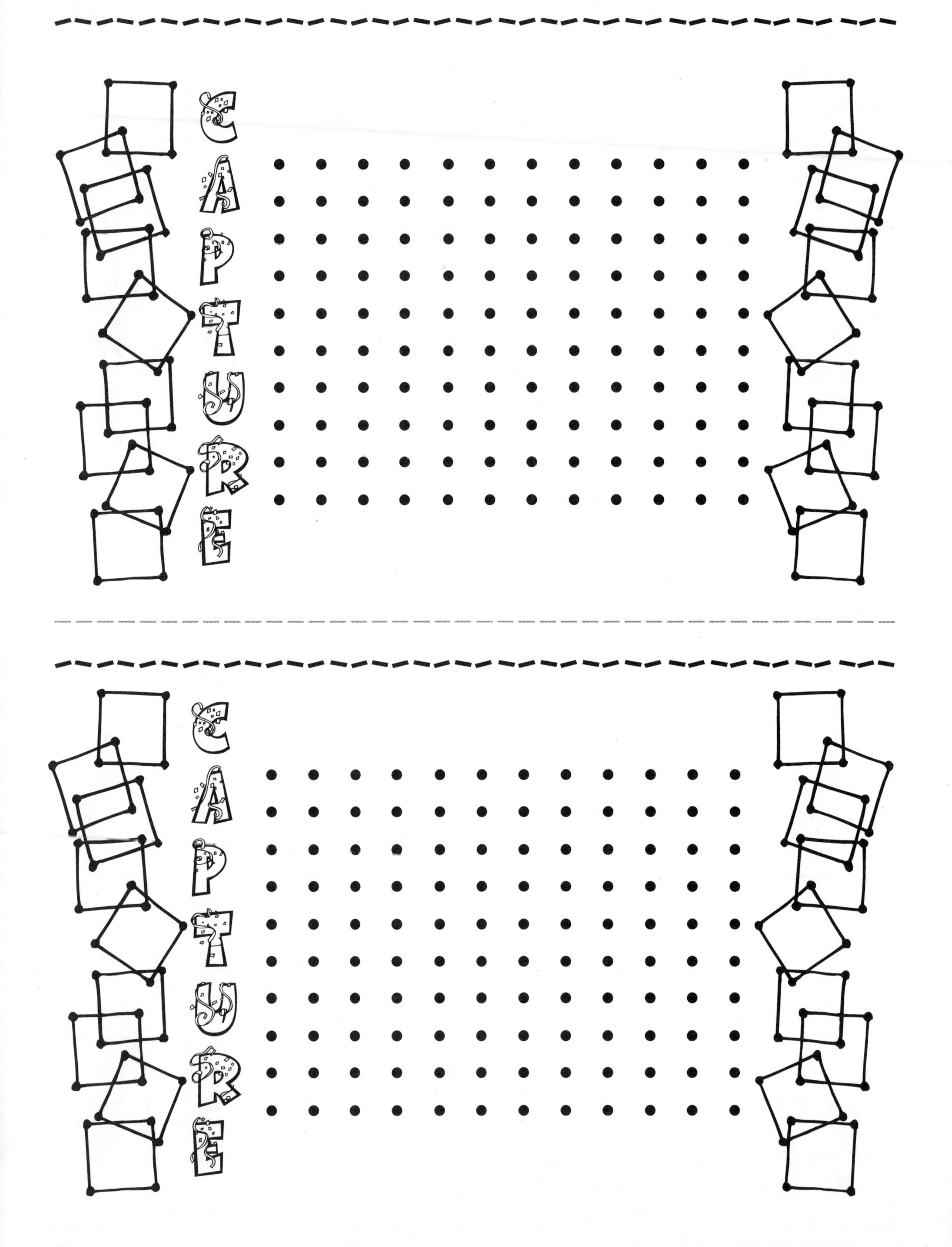
CAPTURE
CAPTURE

# Mosaics

The purpose of this activity is to provide an enhanced tactile experience and practice writing words. The activity can be integrated with other curriculum areas.

**Materials:**
Styrofoam meat trays, scraps of colored paper, scissors, white glue, art books with photographs of mosaics, list of spelling words

**Preparation:**
Ask students and colleagues to bring in clean meat trays from home.

**Activity:**

1. Show the class some photographs of mosaics. Discuss how a picture or design is developed by using small pieces of color.

2. Tell the students that they are each going to create a mosaic. Give each child a meat tray. Point out that the rim of the tray will act as a frame. The students should use the center portion of the tray for the mosaic.

3. Tell the class that they should cut out a number of small pieces for their mosaic from the scraps of colored paper. They should write one spelling word on each piece. Require that each spelling word appear at least twice in the completed project.

4. Encourage students to take time to arrange and rearrange the colored pieces before gluing them to the tray.

# Metal Working

The purpose of this activity is to provide an enhanced tactile experience and practice writing words.

**Materials:**
Heavy-duty aluminum foil, old newspapers, pencils with very dull points, list of spelling words

**Activity:**

1. Give each student one piece of newspaper (it should be a large piece with a center fold and four sides of text). Have the students keep the piece of newsprint folded, then fold it in half top to bottom, and then fold it in half again side to side.

2. Have each student tear off a sheet of aluminum foil that is larger than the folded newsprint. The students should cover their newsprint with the aluminum foil, wrapping the edges of the foil around to the back to provide a smooth front surface.

3. Using the dull pencils, the students should write their spelling words on the foil surface. Be sure they don't press too firmly or they will tear the foil.

4. Once the spelling words have been written, allow students to decorate the foil with additional markings to create a pleasant design. Small dots, sets of short parallel lines, and gentle spirals work well on this project. Small shapes and markings are better "metal working" techniques than large, expressive drawings.

# TOPIC-SPECIFIC ACTIVITIES

## Spelling Rules

When it comes to spelling, our language is filled with inconsistencies and pitfalls. However there are some rules that, once learned, will help students become better spelling practitioners. These rules cover concepts beyond basic phonetics, and are presented in the following pages. Each rule is followed by 20 words that illustrate the concept. Activities are also provided to use with each list. In addition, you may use any of the General Activities with the following spelling lists. Pick and choose both the words and the type of activities that will most benefit your students.

As you read, keep in mind that every rule has exceptions. You may decide to turn these exceptions into a spelling list. Exceptions can be taught as a lesson or added to the "PLUS" section of the students' logbooks (see p. 20). You can even establish an "Exception Squad" to seek out law-breaking words.

## Specialty Lists

Following the section on spelling rules, you will find activities and lists that deal with prefixes and suffixes. Again, 20 words accompany each suffix or prefix to illustrate its use. You may want to use only 10 of the words with fourth graders, but eighth graders should be expected to handle all 20. The lists are geared more toward the upper grades, since fewer spelling materials are available for that level. Each list includes suggested activities for instruction.

By using the specialty lists, the spelling rule lists, and the lists for homophones and spelling demons that follow, you will find you have a year's worth of spelling words that can help you "teach spelling without going crazy!"

## Rule: A q is always followed by a u

**List Option 1**

| | | | |
|---|---|---|---|
| **antique** | **critique** | **quadrant** | **quantity** |
| **queen** | **question** | **quiet** | **quill** |
| **quilt** | **quit** | **quiver** | **quiz** |
| **quota** | **quotation** | **quote** | **quotient** |
| **squad** | **square** | **squeal** | **unique** |

**List Option 2**

| | | | |
|---|---|---|---|
| **clique** | **grotesque** | **quack** | **quadruple** |
| **quaint** | **quake** | **quality** | **quarter** |
| **quench** | **quick** | **quite** | **require** |
| **squash** | **squat** | **squeak** | **squeeze** |
| **squid** | **squirm** | **squirrel** | **technique** |

1. Give students drawing paper, colored pencils, and markers. Ask them to design a logo that illustrates that q and u must always be together. Have the students write a slogan to go along with their logo.

2. Challenge students to discover words that have a q but no u. It will take some determined digging to uncover them, but there are about 20 foreign words that exist.

3. Tell the class that they are to develop a Qu Question Quiz. They are to write a question for each of the spelling words. Have the students exchange quizzes with a classmate and answer the questions.

**Examples:**
What is another word for silence? (quiet)
What do you call a figure with four equal sides and four equal angles? (square)
What is the name of a small tree-dwelling rodent that has thick fur and a bushy tail? (squirrel)
Who is the female monarch of England? (queen)

## Rule: To make a word that ends in s, x, z, ch, or sh plural, add es; for most other words, add s

| | | | |
|---|---|---|---|
| **annexes** | **beaches** | **brushes** | **bushes** |
| **buzzes** | **churches** | **classes** | **coaches** |
| **crashes** | **hoaxes** | **glasses** | **indexes** |
| **marshes** | **mixes** | **passes** | **stitches** |
| **taxes** | **waltzes** | **witches** | **witnesses** |

1. Have the students write each word. Then have them underline the base-word ending s, x, z, ch, or sh with a red pencil. Have them circle all suffixes in blue.

2. Play "What's My Ending?" Give each child a paper numbered 1 to 20 and two small squares of paper. Have the students decorate one square with a large *s*, the other with a bold *es*. Remind students of the plural rule. Then call out a word. Have students hold up their *es* card if the word requires that plural suffix, and hold up the *s* card if that suffix is needed. Continue calling out words, occasionally asking the class to write a word. Students should then correctly spell the word on their numbered paper. The following are some words to get you started. You will, of course, want to include all the spelling base words in the game.

| | | | |
|---|---|---|---|
| eagle | carpet | mover | bus |
| train | rabbit | button | leech |
| angle | star | computer | fizz |
| brick | candle | diamond | caress |
| peach | vote | motor | birch |
| kitten | ranch | tower | school |
| grass | clock | branch | lizard |
| truck | mass | bird | singer |
| joke | tunnel | marsh | pizza |

## Rule: Nouns ending in y after a vowel form the plural by adding s; nouns ending in y after a consonant form the plural by changing the y to i and adding es

**List Option 1**

| | | | |
|---|---|---|---|
| **babies** | **candies** | **chimneys** | **communities** |
| **convoys** | **copies** | **corduroys** | **countries** |
| **diaries** | **dictionaries** | **enemies** | **highways** |
| **hobbies** | **holidays** | **journeys** | **libraries** |
| **monkeys** | **mysteries** | **theories** | **valleys** |

**List Option 2**

| | | | |
|---|---|---|---|
| **alloys** | **berries** | **bullies** | **buoys** |
| **charities** | **counties** | **dairies** | **donkeys** |
| **emergencies** | **envoys** | **missionaries** | **qualities** |
| **replays** | **Saturdays** | **strays** | **Sundays** |
| **tallies** | **tendencies** | **therapies** | **volleys** |

1. Have students write each rule as a column heading. Then have them list the corresponding words under each rule.

2. Tell students to write each word. Then have them circle the *ys* in each word in red and the *ies* in each word in green.

3. Ask students to write each spelling word and then, next to each word, its singular form.

4. Create two posters, one containing each rule. Let students work in groups to find additional words that follow each rule. Have students write their words on the respective posters with brightly colored markers.

## Rule: Most nouns ending in f or fe form the plural by changing the f or fe to v and adding es (for a double f, just add s)

**List Option 1**

| | | | |
|---|---|---|---|
| **calf** | **calves** | **elf** | **elves** |
| **half** | **halves** | **knife** | **knives** |
| **leaf** | **leaves** | **life** | **lives** |
| **loaf** | **loaves** | **shelf** | **shelves** |
| **wife** | **wives** | **wolf** | **wolves** |

**List Option 2**

| | | | |
|---|---|---|---|
| **bluffs** | **cliffs** | **cuffs** | **dwarf** |
| **dwarves** | **hoof** | **hooves** | **puffs** |
| **scarf** | **scarves** | **scuffs** | **self** |
| **selves** | **sheaf** | **sheaves** | **staffs** |
| **thief** | **thieves** | **wharf** | **wharves** |

1. Have the students make puzzle pairs. Give each child 10 strips of colored paper. Have the students print the singular form of the spelling word on the left side of the strip and the plural form on the right hand side. Tell students to carefully cut between the two words to form a pair of puzzle pieces. Let students keep their pieces in an envelope. Have them exchange envelopes with a friend and put the puzzles together.

2. Assign a story-writing project to the class. Require that at least seven spelling words be used in each story. Try the following topics as story starters.

**For List Option 1:**

- Elves and wolves in a magic forest
- The adventurous life of a talking calf
- A missing collection of mysterious knives

**For List Option 2:**

- Magic dwarves living on cliffs
- The adventure of the horse with musical hooves
- The mystery of the thief and the golden scarves

## Rule: Put i before e except after c, or when sounded like a as in neighbor and weigh

**List Option 1**

| | | | |
|---|---|---|---|
| achieve | believe | brief | chief |
| conceited | deceive | eight | fiend |
| fierce | freight | grief | niece |
| perceive | receipt | relief | retrieve |
| review | siege | vein | weigh |

**List Option 2**

| | | | |
|---|---|---|---|
| beliefs | ceiling | conceive | deceit |
| friend | grieving | heir | mischief |
| neighborhood | piece | pier | premiere |
| receive | relieve | reindeer | shield |
| sleigh | view | weight | yield |

1. Tell the students to make three columns on their papers. The heading for the first column should say "i before e," the second column should say "except after c," and the third column "sounds like a." Have the students write each spelling word in the appropriate column.

| i before e | except after c | sounds like a |
|---|---|---|
| achieve | ceiling | weigh |
| relieve | deceive | vein |
| relief | deceit | freight |
| brief | receive | sleigh |
| retrieve | | eight |
| fiend | | |
| mischief | | |
| yield | | |

2. Have students refer to the columns they created in exercise 1. Ask them to choose one of the lists they have formed. Students should then use all of the words in that column to write a paragraph.

**Example (using words that have i before e):**

It is important to believe in yourself in order to achieve your goals. Do not let a fierce siege of brief setbacks be the fiend that keeps you from trying. Do not let grief over defeats cause you to fail. Relax and give yourself relief from stress. Then, retrieve your courage, review your chief goals, and move forward. Whether you are a son or daughter, nephew or niece, keep your eye on your goals and keep trying.

3. Group the students into pairs. Give each pair a small piece of sandpaper and a piece of felt the same size. Also give each pair of students a handful of scrap paper cut into small squares (you can use the backs of old worksheets or construction paper scraps left over from an art project). On the piece of felt, use a marker to write the letters ie. On the sandpaper, use a marker or crayon to write the letters ei. Tell students to look at their first spelling word. Using the squares, the students should write the letters needed (one letter per square) to spell the first word. When they come to an ie they should use the piece of felt. If the word requires the ei combination, they should use the sandpaper. Remind students that they should reuse the letter squares to spell each word and only create new letters as needed. The use of a texture for ie and ei should help students to remember the correct combination. Keep the letter squares and textured pieces in an envelope for future review lessons.

4. Have students write the words in alphabetical order. Next have them write sentences using the words in alphabetical order.

**Example (for List Option 1):**
I achieve my goals because I believe in myself!
I am being brief when I say that chief is very conceited.
He tried to deceive us by saying he was eight years younger than his true age.
The cartoon fiend gave a fierce yell as the freight train ran over his foot.

5. Tell the students that there are some unique exceptions to the i before e rule. Have the students work in groups as "Exception Squads." The groups should search through newspapers, magazines, textbooks, or even the dictionary to find these offending words. After the squads have written a list of these words, discuss them in class, crossing out any duplicates. Have the students create a poster on newsprint that lists the exceptions they found. A few common exceptions are caffeine, counterfeit, efficiency, efficient, and science.

## Rule: If a one-syllable word has a <u>short vowel sound and ends with one consonant</u>, double the final consonant before adding a suffix that begins with a vowel or y

**List Option 1**

| | | | |
|---|---|---|---|
| **biggest** | **bitten** | **clipping** | **dimmer** |
| **dropping** | **flatten** | **funny** | **grinning** |
| **hidden** | **hopping** | **hottest** | **muddy** |
| **quitting** | **rubbed** | **shopper** | **skipped** |
| **starry** | **stepped** | **stubbed** | **sunny** |

**List Option 2**

| | | | |
|---|---|---|---|
| **baggy** | **clapping** | **cupped** | **digging** |
| **fattest** | **flopped** | **funny** | **jammed** |
| **knotted** | **lapped** | **mopping** | **plotting** |
| **rigging** | **rotten** | **scrubber** | **sloppy** |
| **stopped** | **trapper** | **wetter** | **written** |

1. Tell the students to write each word. Have them circle the double consonants in red, underline the base words in blue, and put two yellow lines under each suffix.

2. Provide the class with a large selection of old magazines and newspapers. Have students cut out sets of double letters they find in the spelling words and glue the letters to drawing paper. Then have students write their spelling words using the cut-out letters for the doubled consonants.

3. Have the children make three-part puzzles. Give each student 20 pieces of colored paper. Have students write each spelling word on a different strip of paper. They should then cut the word into three parts. The first section should be the base word, the second section the added consonant, and the third section the suffix. After they have created their puzzles, let the students exchange them with a classmate for reassembly.

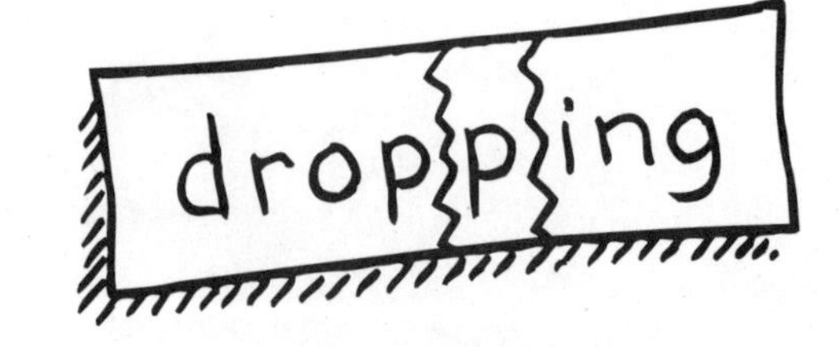

**Rule: If a one-syllable word ends with two consonants or two vowels and one consonant, do not double the final consonant before adding a suffix that begins with a vowel**

**List Option 1**

| | | | |
|---|---|---|---|
| **acting** | **barked** | **beaten** | **blacken** |
| **boiling** | **cheaper** | **coating** | **darken** |
| **frosting** | **loafing** | **neater** | **printer** |
| **sailing** | **signed** | **soiled** | **sticking** |
| **talking** | **thinking** | **waiter** | **wilted** |

**List Option 2**

| | | | |
|---|---|---|---|
| **brushed** | **cheater** | **clicked** | **crusher** |
| **dampen** | **helping** | **hosted** | **picked** |
| **quicker** | **reader** | **rested** | **rocking** |
| **sharpen** | **shocker** | **sleeting** | **sticker** |
| **stinking** | **trained** | **trusted** | **walking** |

1. Ask students to mark their papers with two columns. The first column should be headed "ends with two consonants" and the second column entitled "ends with two vowels and one consonant." Have students write each spelling word under the correct heading.

2. Have students write each spelling word. Then have them circle each base word in green and underline each suffix in purple.

3. Remind students that word families consist of words that rhyme and have most of the same letters. Usually only the first one or two letters change the pattern in word families. Have students write each spelling word and create as large a word family for each word as possible.

**Examples:**
brushed–bushed, crushed, flushed, gushed, hushed, mushed, pushed, rushed, shushed
sticking–clicking, flicking, kicking, licking, nicking, picking, ticking, tricking, wicking

## Rule: If a one-syllable word has a short vowel sound, do not double the final consonant before adding a suffix that begins with a consonant

| | | | |
|---|---|---|---|
| **badly** | **dimly** | **fitness** | **flatly** |
| **fretful** | **gladly** | **hatless** | **jobless** |
| **madly** | **madness** | **manly** | **redness** |
| **sadly** | **sadness** | **sinful** | **skinless** |
| **thinly** | **wetness** | **winless** | **witness** |

1. Have the students write each word. Then have them put a red line under each base word and circle each suffix in blue.

2. Begin a class poster for a word collection. Write the above rule at the top of the poster. Let students add a word each time they find one that correctly follows the rule.

3. Play Memory Chain. In this game, players must repeat whatever letters have been said before them and then add the next letter to the word. Make it clear to the class in which order each child is to speak. It is easiest to move up and down each row, through the room, in serpentine fashion. If you have table groups, move clockwise around the table and then clockwise around the room.

To play, the teacher announces the word to be spelled. The first student says the first letter, the second student says the first letter and adds the second letter, and so on until the word is complete. If someone makes a mistake, then the chain is broken and a new word is started by the next student.

**Example:** If the first word is thinly, the game should proceed in this way:

student 1: t
student 2: t-h
student 3: t-h-i
student 4: t-h-i-n
student 5: t-h-i-n-l
student 6: t-h-i-n-l-y
student 7: would begin the next word

## Rule: Drop a silent e before adding a suffix that begins with a vowel

| | | | |
|---|---|---|---|
| **balanced** | **believing** | **caring** | **continuation** |
| **creative** | **dancing** | **declaration** | **expensive** |
| **intensive** | **motivation** | **quotation** | **relieved** |
| **repulsive** | **retrieving** | **revolving** | **shaken** |
| **sharing** | **surfaced** | **telephoned** | **trembling** |

1. Remind the class how to set up mathematical equations. Write several on the board. Tell students that they are going to write equations for each of the spelling words. They must first write the base word, then show the subtraction of the e, and then the addition of the suffix.

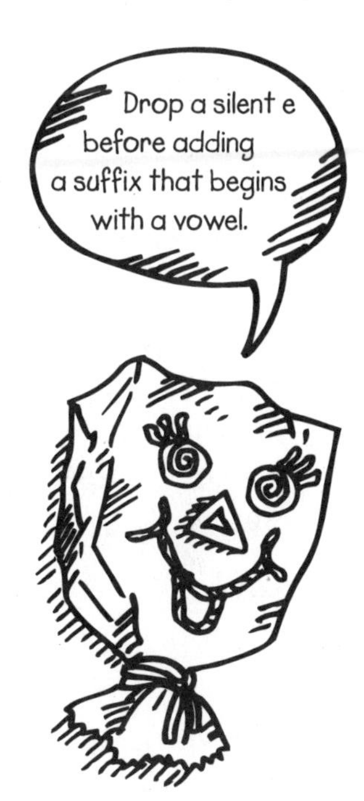


**Examples:**
surface - e + ed = surfaced
motivate - e + ation = motivation

2. Have students write 10 spelling sentences using two different spelling words in each sentence.

3. Divide the class into groups. Tell the students that each group is to think of a short skit to perform for the class. The skit should teach the spelling rule. Let the students choose whether they want to act out the skit themselves or design and use puppets to make the presentation. Provide colored paper, yarn, grocery bags, craft sticks, foil, poster board, and scraps of material for students to make into puppets or props.

## Rule: If a word ends with silent e, do not drop the e when adding a suffix that begins with a consonant

| | | | |
|---|---|---|---|
| **accurately** | **achievement** | **amusement** | **announcement** |
| **bravely** | **disgraceful** | **engagement** | **enlargement** |
| **extremely** | **genuinely** | **hopeful** | **immediately** |
| **intensely** | **likeness** | **management** | **replacement** |
| **ripeness** | **sincerely** | **tasteless** | **wasteful** |

1. Have students write each base word in green, write each suffix in blue, and circle each silent e in red.

2. Host a Scavenger Hunt. Divide the class into groups of two or three. Let the groups search books, magazines, and other written material for additional words that follow the pattern. After a set time period, let each group read their words. Other groups should cross off any words that they also have on their lists. Award a prize to the group that comes up with the most words.

3. Assign an essay on one of the following topics. Remind students to use as many of the spelling words in their essays as possible. Ask students to underline the spelling words in their assignment.

- Management of Study Time
- Achievement in the World of Sports
- Babysitter's Amusement Guide for Small Children
- Recognizing Tasteless Fashions
- How to Bravely Remain Hopeful
- How to Accurately Judge the Ripeness of Fruit

## Rule: The sound of /shun/ is usually spelled -tion, and less often -sion

**List Option 1**

| | | | |
|---|---|---|---|
| automation | celebration | composition | conclusion |
| congregation | conversion | deduction | description |
| direction | examination | exhaustion | extension |
| frustration | function | information | invasion |
| motion | multiplication | tension | transportation |

**List Option 2**

| | | | |
|---|---|---|---|
| auction | caption | conversation | correction |
| dimension | division | explanation | fictional |
| fraction | international | introduction | invention |
| mission | multiplication | rational | relaxation |
| retention | revision | rotation | traction |

1. Have the students write each word. Then have them circle all -tion words in orange and all -sion words in blue.

2. Discuss with the class the fact that most of the spelling words are nouns. Have students add a verb or another word or two to each spelling word to create a phrase.

> **Examples:**
> understand the function
> pass the examination
> complete the mission

3. Have students write rhyming couplets using two spelling words in each small poem.

> **Examples:**
> I am always filled with total frustration
> When I don't get the correct information!
>
> Looking into the future with great celebration,
> Homework may be done by robot automation.

## Rule: When the suffix -ly is added to a word, the spelling of the base word does not usually change

| | | | |
|---|---|---|---|
| **actively** | **anxiously** | **boldly** | **clearly** |
| **creatively** | **definitely** | **graciously** | **joyfully** |
| **kindly** | **neatly** | **quickly** | **quietly** |
| **rapidly** | **rudely** | **shyly** | **slowly** |
| **softly** | **swiftly** | **totally** | **wisely** |

1. Introduce Tom Swifties by sharing the following information with the class.

Tom Swift was a young adventure-book hero created by E. Stratemeyer. During the early 1900s, Stratemeyer's adventure stories were very popular with children. Tom and his friends never just said something. Instead, they said it boldly, quietly, or softly. Today, Tom Swifties are adverb quotations that result in a pun. What is said corresponds with how it is said.

Discuss the following examples with the class. Then have the students write a Tom Swiftie for each of the spelling words.

**Examples:**
"White water rafting is awesome," said Tom rapidly.
"The window is all clean," said Tom clearly.
"The figures in the addition problem are correct," Tom agreed totally.

2. Provide magazines and newspapers for the class. Have students cut out photographs, drawings, or comics that in some way correspond to their spelling words. Students should then write a phrase for each picture. You may wish to have students glue the pictures to drawing paper and then write the phrases beneath each one. Another option is to number the pictures and then number the written phrases accordingly.

## Rule: The suffix -ful never has two ls; when -ful is added to a word, the spelling of the base word usually does not change

| | | | |
|---|---|---|---|
| **careful** | **cheerful** | **colorful** | **delightful** |
| **distasteful** | **forceful** | **graceful** | **grateful** |
| **harmful** | **helpful** | **insightful** | **masterful** |
| **meaningful** | **peaceful** | **playful** | **powerful** |
| **sorrowful** | **stressful** | **tearful** | **vengeful** |

1. Have students write each word. Have them underline each base word in blue and circle each suffix in purple.

2. Give students drawing paper and markers or colored pencils. Have them design a symbol that will remind them that the suffix -ful never has two ls. Have students staple their symbol to a page in their logbooks.

3. Have students write descriptive sentences about the personality traits of famous people, fictional characters, or superheroes or other cartoon characters. Each sentence should include a spelling word. Remind students to underline the spelling word in each sentence.

**Examples:**
Sherlock Holmes is always insightful.
Princess Diana was lovely and graceful.
Sammy Sosa is a powerful home run hitter.

**Rule: If a word ends with a consonant and a y, change the y to i before adding any suffix except one that begins with i; do not change the y if it is preceded by a vowel**

| | | | |
|---|---|---|---|
| **beautiful** | **cried** | **defiant** | **displayed** |
| **employer** | **enjoyed** | **fliers** | **fried** |
| **happiness** | **healthier** | **heavily** | **joyful** |
| **merciful** | **mysterious** | **playful** | **pliable** |
| **sleepiness** | **steadily** | **studious** | **victorious** |

1. Have students write each spelling word and each matching base word.

2. Tell the class to create two columns on a piece of paper. The heading of the first column should be "Change y to i"; the title on the other column should be "Don't change the y." Have the students write each spelling word in the correct column. Then divide the class into pairs. Let each pair search through the newspaper to find at least 20 more words that fit the categories.

3. Assign a writing project on one of the following topics. Require students to use at least seven spelling words in their essays. Remind the class to underline any spelling words they use. Give bonus points for using words from a previous list.

- Ways to make healthier food choices
- What it means to be beautiful
- Ten things to make life more joyful
- Happiness is . . .
- What makes champions victorious
- Ways to make a story mysterious

## Rule: When a word ends with a y, do not change the y when adding a suffix beginning with i

| | | | |
|---|---|---|---|
| **applying** | **complying** | **crying** | **defying** |
| **drying** | **employing** | **enjoying** | **flying** |
| **fortifying** | **paying** | **pitying** | **praying** |
| **relying** | **spying** | **staying** | **steadying** |
| **studying** | **supplying** | **tallying** | **trying** |

1. Have the students write each spelling word. Then have them underline each base word in blue, circle each y in red, and box each suffix in yellow.

2. Have students, one at a time, come up and act out one of the spelling words. The class may guess the answer, but the answer must be **spelled**, not spoken.

3. Assign one of the following writing topics. Require that students use at least 10 of the spelling words in their assignment. Remind the class to underline the spelling words they use.

- A Very Scary Airplane Ride
- What I Did This Weekend
- Tips for a Day at the Mall
- Babysitting the Horrible Child
- Extreme Sports in My Yard

## Prefix re-: The prefix re- means again, anew, or back; when adding this prefix, the spelling of the base word does not change

| | | | |
|---|---|---|---|
| **react** | **rearrange** | **recover** | **recycle** |
| **refill** | **refinish** | **reform** | **refund** |
| **release** | **remake** | **remind** | **remove** |
| **replace** | **replay** | **rerun** | **restart** |
| **return** | **reuse** | **review** | **rewrite** |

1. Write each spelling word on a small slip of paper. Place the slips in a box or basket. Have a student come forward, choose a slip, and then act out the word. Let the class guess which word is being acted out. The person who guesses correctly spells the word aloud.

2. Give the class an essay-writing assignment on one of the following topics. Require students to use at least 10 spelling words in their essays.

- How to reuse, refinish, or recycle something
- Ways to repair, recover, or remake an old item into something new
- Why sports officials should or should not use instant replay to review their judgments
- The reasons why I would like to reform a certain school rule

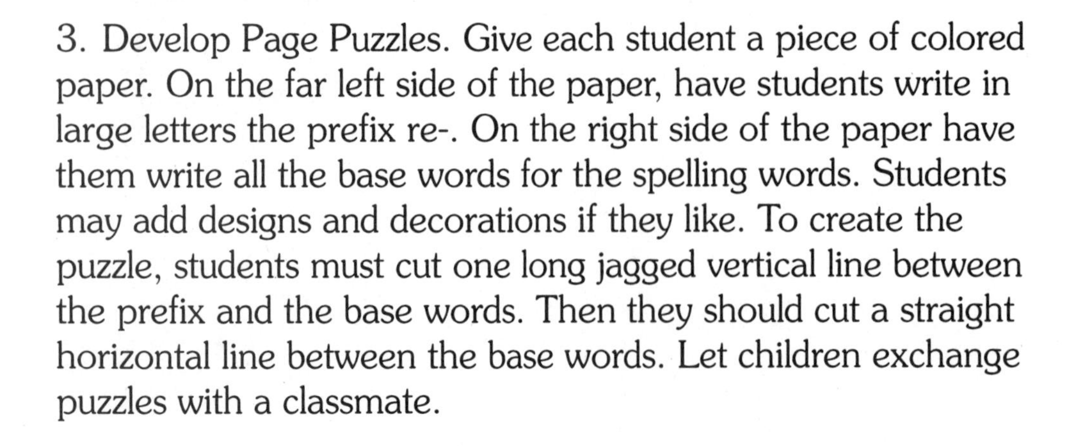

3. Develop Page Puzzles. Give each student a piece of colored paper. On the far left side of the paper, have students write in large letters the prefix re-. On the right side of the paper have them write all the base words for the spelling words. Students may add designs and decorations if they like. To create the puzzle, students must cut one long jagged vertical line between the prefix and the base words. Then they should cut a straight horizontal line between the base words. Let children exchange puzzles with a classmate.

## Prefixes dis- and mis- : The prefixes dis- and mis- mean opposite, wrong, or absence of; when adding this prefix, the spelling of the base word does not change

**List Option 1**

| | | | |
|---|---|---|---|
| **disability** | **disagree** | **disappointed** | **discard** |
| **disconnect** | **discourage** | **dismount** | **dispose** |
| **disregard** | **disrespect** | **misadventure** | **miscalculated** |
| **misdemeanor** | **misfire** | **misgivings** | **misleading** |
| **misplace** | **misrepresent** | **mistreat** | **misunderstanding** |

**List Option 2**

| | | | |
|---|---|---|---|
| **disable** | **disappear** | **disapprove** | **discomfort** |
| **discount** | **disgrace** | **dismiss** | **displeased** |
| **disrepair** | **dissatisfied** | **misbehave** | **misconduct** |
| **misdirect** | **misfortune** | **misinterpret** | **mismatch** |
| **misquote** | **misread** | **misspell** | **mistrust** |

1. Have students write each word. Then have them trace over each prefix with a red pencil and underline each base word in blue. If there is a suffix, they should circle it in green.

2. Give students one of the following subjects for a writing assignment. Require that students use at least eight spelling words in their essays.

- An occasion when I was disappointed or dissatisfied
- How a misunderstanding can happen if something is misread or misspelled
- When adventure turns into misadventure
- A policy with which I disagree
- How to overcome a disability
- Why some people disapprove of today's hit music

## Prefix un- : The prefix un- means not or the reverse of; when adding this prefix, the spelling of the base word does not change

**List Option 1**

| | | | |
|---|---|---|---|
| **unaware** | **unbalanced** | **unbearable** | **unbutton** |
| **unclear** | **uncover** | **uneasy** | **uneven** |
| **unfair** | **unfortunate** | **unhappy** | **unkind** |
| **unleash** | **unload** | **unlucky** | **unnatural** |
| **unplug** | **unreal** | **unsure** | **unusual** |

**List Option 2**

| | | | |
|---|---|---|---|
| **unable** | **unbeaten** | **uncertain** | **uncommon** |
| **uncut** | **unequal** | **unfit** | **unfold** |
| **unfriendly** | **unhealthy** | **unknown** | **unlike** |
| **unlock** | **unnecessary** | **unpack** | **unprepared** |
| **unroll** | **untwist** | **unwind** | **unworthy** |

1. Have students write each word, then underline each base word in green and circle each prefix in orange. If a word has a suffix, the students should trace over it in red.

2. Tell students to write "If . . . then . . ." sentences. The "If" phrase in the sentence should indicate the meaning of a spelling word, and the "then" portion must contain the underlined word.

**Examples:**
If a food is not good for your blood pressure, then it is unhealthy.
If I want you to open the newspaper, then I will ask you to unfold it.

3. Make Reverse Books. Give each child 20 small squares of paper. Have students put all squares in a stack and staple the left side to form a booklet. On the front side of each page, the students should write a spelling word. Have the students flip their books over, vertically, so that the staples remain on the left side. Students now write base words for the spelling words. When they read the book in one direction, they will see the base words; when they read it in the other direction they will see the spelling words.

## Prefix pre- : The prefix pre- means before; when adding this prefix the spelling of the base word does not change

| | | | |
|---|---|---|---|
| **preamble** | **precaution** | **precede** | **precook** |
| **prefer** | **preheat** | **prejudice** | **prelude** |
| **premature** | **premeditated** | **premonition** | **prenatal** |
| **prepaid** | **prepare** | **preschool** | **preshrunk** |
| **presume** | **pretest** | **prevent** | **preview** |

1. Point out to the class that a prefix is added on at the beginning of a word. Have students write each spelling word, then circle the prefix in green.

2. Have students look up the definition of each of their spelling words in the dictionary. They should then write each word in a sentence, explaining how it relates to the meaning **before**.

**Examples:**
The baby was born before the due date, so it was premature.
You must precook the sausage in a skillet before you add it to that casserole.
To judge people before you get to know them is a sign of prejudice.

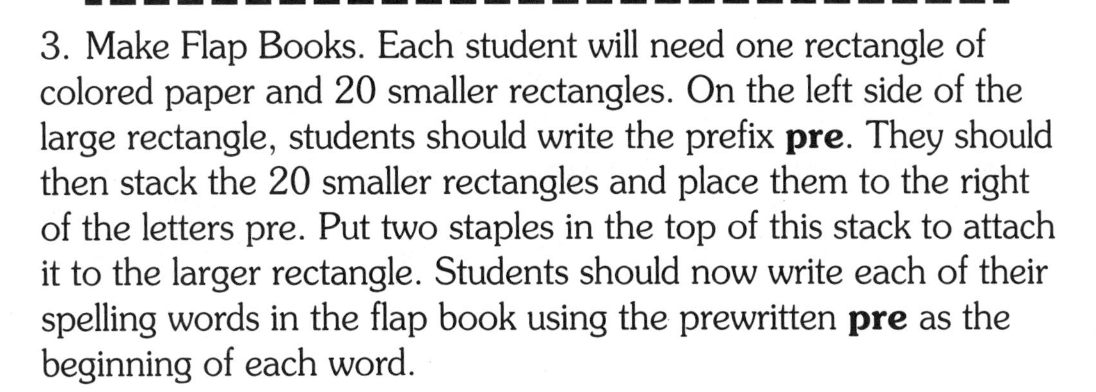

3. Make Flap Books. Each student will need one rectangle of colored paper and 20 smaller rectangles. On the left side of the large rectangle, students should write the prefix **pre**. They should then stack the 20 smaller rectangles and place them to the right of the letters pre. Put two staples in the top of this stack to attach it to the larger rectangle. Students should now write each of their spelling words in the flap book using the prewritten **pre** as the beginning of each word.

## Numeric Prefixes: These prefixes give number value to a word: mono- and uni- mean one, bi- means two, tri- means three, and quad- means four

**List Option 1**

| | | | |
|---|---|---|---|
| **biceps** | **bicycle** | **bifocals** | **bilingual** |
| **monochrome** | **monocle** | **monogram** | **monolith** |
| **quadrant** | **quadruple** | **triceps** | **trifold** |
| **trio** | **triple** | **unicorn** | **unicycle** |
| **unify** | **union** | **unit** | **universal** |

**List Option 2**

| | | | |
|---|---|---|---|
| **binary** | **bipartisan** | **biplane** | **biracial** |
| **monologue** | **monopoly** | **monorail** | **monotone** |
| **quadruplets** | **triangle** | **tricycle** | **triplets** |
| **triplicate** | **tripod** | **uniform** | **unique** |
| **unison** | **united** | **unity** | **universe** |

1. Have students write each word that means one once, each word that means two twice, each word that means three three times, and each word that means four four times.

2. Tell the class to look up each of the spelling words in the dictionary. Then have them write each word in a sentence. Each sentence should include the number that corresponds to the prefix (see examples that follow). Have students underline both the spelling word and the number in each sentence.

**Examples:**

The <u>universe</u> is the <u>one</u> thing that includes every other thing.

Computers use a <u>binary</u> system based on only <u>two</u> numbers.

We had to purchase <u>three</u> toys for the <u>triplets</u>.

## Between -able and -ible Part I: If the base word is whole, the suffix is usually spelled -able; the silent e is dropped from the base word before adding this suffix

**List Option 1**

| | | | |
|---|---|---|---|
| **acceptable** | **accountable** | **allowable** | **breakable** |
| **chewable** | **commendable** | **dependable** | **enjoyable** |
| **fashionable** | **laughable** | **playable** | **reasonable** |
| **refundable** | **returnable** | **stackable** | **unbearable** |
| **untouchable** | **washable** | **wearable** | **workable** |

**List Option 2**

| | | | |
|---|---|---|---|
| **achievable** | **admirable** | **adorable** | **believable** |
| **conceivable** | **consumable** | **curable** | **deplorable** |
| **desirable** | **disposable** | **excitable** | **imaginable** |
| **livable** | **measurable** | **movable** | **observable** |
| **perceivable** | **pleasurable** | **recyclable** | **usable** |

1. Have the students create Word Arithmetic statements for each spelling word.

**Examples:**
accept + able = acceptable
measure – e + able = measurable

2. Have the students write "If . . .then . . ." sentences. The spelling word should appear in one phrase of the sentence and the base word in the other.

**Examples:**
If the plan will work, then it is workable.
If the scientist can observe an atom, then it is observable.

## Between -able and -ible Part II: When the base word is incomplete or a root, the suffix is usually spelled -ible

| | | | |
|---|---|---|---|
| **admissible** | **audible** | **combustible** | **compatible** |
| **divisible** | **edible** | **eligible** | **feasible** |
| **horrible** | **incredible** | **invisible** | **legible** |
| **permissible** | **plausible** | **possible** | **responsible** |
| **susceptible** | **tangible** | **terrible** | **visible** |

1. Have students write each word, then circle each suffix in red.

2. Divide the class into partners or small groups. Have the groups create ads for imaginary products. Each ad should include a picture of the product and text that uses at least seven spelling words.

> **Example:**
> Incredible, edible Dynamite Gum! The flavor is responsible for your mouth feeling combustible!!!! Don't settle for horrible gum with terrible flavor. Explosive flavor is possible with Dynamite Gum!

3. Let students choose from among the following story starters. Have them develop a story that includes at least 10 of their spelling words. Remind students to underline those words in their writing.

> - Yesterday I woke up to discover I was invisible.
> - I was taking out the garbage when I saw something horrible.
> - Sitting in my room I heard something barely audible coming from inside the walls.
> - I think my little brother/sister is combustible.
> - My incredible trip to ________!
> - The most terrible day of my life was. . .

## Suffixes -dom and -ship: These suffixes mean state of being; when adding them, the spelling of the base word does not usually change

| | | | |
|---|---|---|---|
| **boredom** | **championship** | **citizenship** | **craftsmanship** |
| **dictatorship** | **freedom** | **friendship** | **horsemanship** |
| **kingdom** | **kinship** | **marksmanship** | **martyrdom** |
| **ownership** | **partnership** | **scholarship** | **sponsorship** |
| **sportsmanship** | **stardom** | **stewardship** | **workmanship** |

1. Have the students write each word twice. Then have them use a light colored marker to highlight each suffix.

2. Ask the students to choose one of the spelling words. Tell them that they will develop a project that uses the spelling word as the theme. Give bonus points for every spelling word used in the final project. Following are several ideas for projects, but the children will have some wonderful ideas of their own.

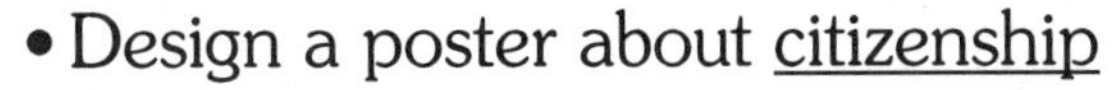

- Design a poster about citizenship
- Create several greeting cards about friendship
- Draw a map of an imaginary kingdom
- Write a newspaper-style article about your favorite team winning a championship
- Design a poster about our stewardship of the environment
- Make a collage of pictures that show craftsmanship
- Write an essay about freedom
- Write a poem about boredom
- Research ways to earn a scholarship—make a list of helpful hints
- Draw a set of comic strips about sportsmanship
- Develop a magazine article about the responsibilities of pet ownership

## Suffix -less: The suffix -less means without; when adding this suffix, the base word does not usually change

**List Option 1**

| | | | |
|---|---|---|---|
| **airless** | **bottomless** | **boundless** | **breathless** |
| **childless** | **clueless** | **flightless** | **groundless** |
| **heartless** | **hopeless** | **lifeless** | **mindless** |
| **motionless** | **nameless** | **odorless** | **pointless** |
| **senseless** | **speechless** | **thoughtless** | **toothless** |

**List Option 2**

| | | | |
|---|---|---|---|
| **blameless** | **colorless** | **effortless** | **emotionless** |
| **fearless** | **friendless** | **hairless** | **homeless** |
| **joyless** | **matchless** | **meaningless** | **noiseless** |
| **painless** | **peerless** | **seamless** | **sleepless** |
| **strapless** | **timeless** | **useless** | **wireless** |

1. Have students write each word. Then have them underline each base word in red and circle each suffix in blue.

2. Have students write a magazine article on one of the following subjects. Require that at least five spelling words be used in the assignment. When all the articles have been edited, put the final copies together in a class magazine. Let students create pictures to go along with their articles.

- Ways to help the homeless
- How to get rest if you have been sleepless
- How to turn useless junk into matchless treasures
- What to do if you find yourself clueless and speechless
- The best way to handle thoughtless people

3. As a class, discuss some signs and symbols that mean "no." Ask students to think about signs they have seen. Point out that these signs often picture an action and indicate "no" by slashing through the action with a red line. Have students create a symbol in a circle with a slash to represent the meaning of each word.

## Suffixes -er and -or: The suffixes -er and -or mean one who; when adding these suffixes, follow the rules for adding a suffix that begins with a vowel

**List Option 1**

| | | | |
|---|---|---|---|
| aggressor | auditor | conductor | creator |
| director | driver | educator | interviewer |
| manager | operator | oppressor | photographer |
| producer | professor | programmer | protester |
| supervisor | teacher | trainer | writer |

**List Option 2**

| | | | |
|---|---|---|---|
| actor | climber | creditor | defender |
| governor | interpreter | inventor | juggler |
| landowner | legislator | preacher | pretender |
| protector | provider | reviewer | sailor |
| seller | senator | singer | winner |

1. Have students write a complete sentence for each word using the phrase "one who."

**Examples:**
A governor is one who governs a state.
An auditor is one who audits the accounts of a business.

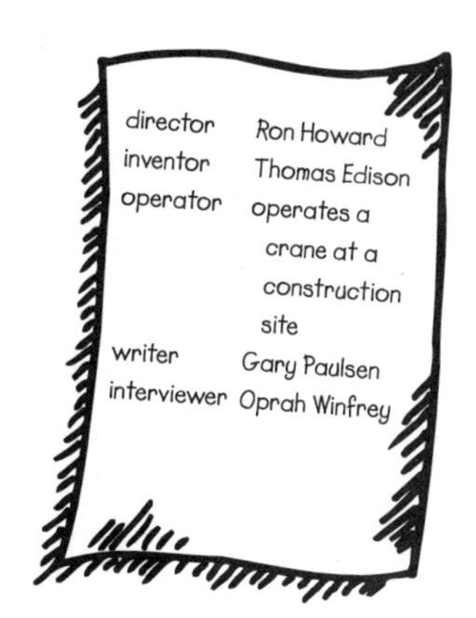


2. Point out that all of the spelling words are terms that describe people. Have students write each spelling word. Following each word, have the students list the name of a person who fits the description. If they are unable to come up with an actual name, have them list where this person might be found.

**Examples:**
director—Ron Howard writer—Gary Paulsen
inventor—Thomas Edison interviewer—Oprah Winfrey
operator—operates a crane at a construction site

## Suffix -ize: The suffix -ize means to do or to make; it may be added to a base word or a root

| | | | |
|---|---|---|---|
| **agonize** | **apologize** | **authorize** | **civilize** |
| **criticize** | **emphasize** | **fertilize** | **harmonize** |
| **jeopardize** | **legalize** | **modernize** | **neutralize** |
| **organize** | **patronize** | **realize** | **scrutinize** |
| **specialize** | **summarize** | **symbolize** | **utilize** |

1. Have students write each word, then circle each suffix in green.

2. Have students write a definition for each word that includes the base word or root.

**Examples:**
criticize—to be a critic; act critical
summarize—to condense information into a summary
apologize—to make an apology

3. Discuss with the class some fun ways to use the -ize ending. Brainstorm as a group some made-up words and their definitions that use this suffix. The whole activity should be done verbally, since the made-up words would involve some creative spelling.

**Examples:**
"carryoutize"—to get Chinese food for dinner
"perfumize"—to spray oneself with perfume or cologne
"musicize"—to add music to any situation

4. Have students write an essay on one of the following topics. Require the use of at least five spelling words in the assignment.

- How to <u>organize</u> your study time
- The best way to <u>apologize</u> after you have <u>criticized</u> someone
- Steps needed to <u>summarize</u> a report
- Ways to <u>fertilize</u> a garden
- The best way to <u>utilize</u> your talents
- New ideas about how to <u>modernize</u> the community

## Suffix -ance: The suffix -ance means action or quality of; it may be added to a base word or root

| | | | |
|---|---|---|---|
| **acceptance** | **acquaintance** | **admittance** | **alliance** |
| **annoyance** | **attendance** | **brilliance** | **elegance** |
| **endurance** | **fragrance** | **grievance** | **guidance** |
| **hindrance** | **insurance** | **maintenance** | **observance** |
| **reluctance** | **remembrance** | **resistance** | **significance** |

1. Have students write each word twice. Then have them use a light colored marker to highlight each suffix.

2. Tell the students that you realize they must follow many rules every day. Let the class share some of the rules they are asked to follow. Tell the students that today they will have a chance to create some wacky rules. They are to write one rule for each spelling word, underlining the spelling word in each sentence. When they're completed, place all the rules in a folder or staple them into book form. Leave the folder at the reading center for free time enjoyment.

> **Examples:**
> Make the acquaintance of someone new each Tuesday that has an even numbered date.
> All guidance counselors must sit in on boring classes at least once a week.
> Locker interiors must be shined to a glossy brilliance every Friday.

3. Make Page Puzzles. Each student will need one sheet of colored paper. On the right side of their paper, students should write in large letters the suffix -ance. On the left side of the paper they should write the base word or root for each spelling word. To make the puzzle, have the students cut one very jagged line down the center of the paper. Next, have them cut horizontally between the base words or roots. Tell the students to exchange puzzles with a friend and solve them.

# Words That Sound and Look Alike

In addition to other confusing elements, the English language throws us for a loop by including a number of words that sound and look alike but have very different meanings. Homographs, homonyms, and homophones provide us with enough confusing similarities and differences to make our heads swim.

Homographs are words that are spelled the same but have different pronunciations and meanings.

lead–an element often used to manufacture ammunition: "The cowboys used lead to make their bullets."
lead–to direct an activity or a group: "Julie will lead the aerobics class."

Homonyms are words that are spelled the same but have differing meanings.

**Example:**
face–confront: "You must face your fear of spiders."
face–frontal portion of the head containing features: "The baby has pudding smeared all over his face."
face–surface layer of an object: "The face of that cabinet is scratched."
face–contortion of the facial features: "Teenagers often make a face when asked to do a household chore."

Homophones are words that are pronounced alike but spelled differently. The words also have very dissimilar meanings. Homophones often give the speller problems. This is especially true when the words' spellings are similar. Homophones may come in pairs or even triplets.

**Examples:**

ant–small insect that lives in a colony: "An ant always seems to know how to find picnic food."
aunt–the sister of one's mother or father: "My mother and my aunt look very much alike, and both enjoy music."

pair–two of something: "You will need a clean pair of socks."
pear–a sweet fruit: "A baked pear with chocolate sauce is a fancy dessert."
pare–peel or cut back: "Pare the apple before using it in that recipe."

Confusion not only reigns when trying to spell or use homophones, homographs, and homonyms, but also in attempting to categorize them. In recent years, the term homonym has become the generic term for all three types of words. Since homographs and homonyms do not challenge the student in spelling, this book will deal only with homophones.

On the next few pages, you will find a variety of activities that can be used when working with homophones that will help clear up some of the confusion for your spellers. The activities are followed by a list of homophones you can use with them. You can also compile customized spelling lists for your class by picking and choosing among sets of homophones.

# Homophone Activities

1. Have students write a pair of sentences that show understanding of a pair of homophones.

> **Example:**
> A piece from the broken pane of glass cut my arm.
> I felt great pain.

2. Divide the class into groups. Let each group come up with mnemonic devices that will help students remember the spellings and meanings of pairs of homophones. Tell students to think about the definitions, then look for letters or groups of letters that will help them remember which spelling goes with each meaning. Share some examples with the class before asking students to write their own mnemonic devices.

> **Examples:**
> stationery–envelopes
> stationary–lack of action
>
> principal–the principal of the school can be your pal
> principle –is a rule or basic truth

3. Hold a relay race. Divide the class into three or four groups. Clearly mark each team's writing space on the chalkboard. Have the first player from each team go to the board. Give two clues to indicate which pair of homophones the students should write. The team that spells the words correctly first, in the proper order, receives 2 points. Any other team with a correct answer receives 1 point. Play continues until each player has at least two turns. Here are some samples of clues that you can use:

> - flew high in the air; a sharp metallic weapon (soared, sword)
> - the yellow of an egg; harness on an ox (yolk, yoke)
> - small glass container; something evil (vial, vile)

4. Play the Memory Game. Cut 20 index cards in half. On one half write a homophone. On the other half write the definition. Lay all the cards out on a table in a grid pattern. The first player turns over two cards. If the word and definition match, the player keeps the cards and takes another turn. If the word and definition do not match, the cards are returned to their original positions and play moves to the next player. Play continues until all the cards have been matched.

5. Have the students write poetry in couplets. Remind students that couplets are composed of two lines, and that the last word of each line rhymes with the last word of the other line. Have the students write couplets with a pair of homophones for the rhyming words.

**Examples:**

There once was a queen whose reign
Was dampened by forty days of rain.

I climbed up the mountain to see
If I could sight the deep, blue sea!

6. Have students carefully study each pair of homophones you choose. Then have them write the first homophone of a pair. Have them write the second word of the pair in this way: with a regular pencil for each letter that is also found in the first word, and with a red pencil for each letter that is different. Have them do this for each pair on the list.

**Examples:**

capitol–capit**al**
patience–patien**ts**
slay–s**leigh**
vice–vi**se**

7. Have the class make Crazy Combos. Tell the children that Crazy Combos are formed by pairing two individual words. Let the students develop these two-word phrases by combining two sets of homophones. After they have created the words, have students draw pictures to illustrate them, or write silly definitions for each combo.

**Examples:**
flour boy–child assistant who measures flour for a baker
buoy flower–unusual blooming plant that grows on harbor markers

8. Let students create flash cards for confusing homophone pairs. Pass out index cards. On one side of the card, students should draw a picture to illustrate a homophone. Students should print the word that the picture represents on the reverse side of the card. Require that each student make cards for at least five pairs of words. Have the class work in pairs to test each other. One child shows another the picture and asks that child to spell the correct word.

9. Have the students make Shape Shifters. Give each child a piece of drawing paper. Ask the students to choose a set of homophones and see what kind of picture comes to mind for each word. Then tell the children to think of a shape that represents each word. Have them use crayons or markers to draw an outline of each shape. Then have them print each corresponding word several times inside the shape. Tell students that they may write the words to follow the contours of each shape.

# Homophone List

**A**
acts, ax
affect, effect
air, heir
aisle, I'll, isle
allowed, aloud
altar, alter
ant, aunt
ate, eight

**B**
bail, bale
ball, bawl
bare, bear
bazaar, bizarre
been, bin
berry, bury
birth, berth
board, bored
bow, bough
boy, buoy
by, bye, buy

**C**
cache, cash
capital, capitol
carrot, karat
cast, caste
ceiling, sealing
cell, sell
cent, scent, sent
cents, scents, sense
chased, chaste
chord, cord, cored
chute, shoot
cite, sight, site
close, clothes
coarse, course
colonel, kernel
council, counsel
coward, cowered
creak, creek
cue, queue
cymbal, symbol

**D**
dear, deer
dense, dents
dew, do, due
die, dye
doe, dough
dual, duel

**E**
earn, urn
ewes, use, yews
eye, I
eyed, I'd

**F**
fair, fare
feat, feet
find, fined
fir, fur
flea, flee
flew, flue
flour, flower
for, fore, four
foul, fowl
frays, phrase
friar, fryer

**G**
gnu, knew, new
gored, gourd
grate, great
groan, grown
guessed, guest

**H**
hair, hare
heal, heel
hear, here
heard, herd
higher, hire
him, hymn
hoarse, horse
hole, whole
hour, our

**I**
idle, idol

**J**
jam, jamb

**K**
knead, need
knight, night
knot, not
know, no
knows, nose

**L**
lead, led
leak, leek
liar, lyre
links, lynx
loan, lone

**M**
made, maid
mail, male
main, mane
manner, manor
marry, merry
marshal, martial
might, mite
mince, mints
miner, minor
moan, mown
muscles, mussels

**N**
naval, navel
none, nun

**O**
oar, or, ore
ode, owed
one, won

**P**
paced, paste
packed, pact
pail, pale
pain, pane
pair, pare, pear
patience, patients
pause, paws
peace, piece
peak, peek
peal, peel
peer, pier
plain, plane

plait, plate
pleas, please
praise, prays, preys
presence, presents
pride, pried
prince, prints
principal, principle
profit, prophet

**Q**

quarts, quartz

**R**

rain, reign, rein
raise, rays, raze
rap, wrap
read, red
read, reed
real, reel
residence, residents
right, rite, write
ring, wring
road, rode, rowed
rose, rows
rye, wry

**S**

sail, sale
scene, seen
scull, skull
sea, see
sew, so, sow
shear, sheer
side, sighed
sighs, size
slay, sleigh
soar, sore
soared, sword
sole, soul
some, sum
son, sun
stairs, stares
stake, steak
stationary,
stationery
steal, steel
straight, strait
suede, swayed

**T**

tacks, tax
tail, tale
taper, tapir
taught, taut
tear, tier
tense, tents
their, there, they're
threw, through
throne, thrown
thyme, time
to, too, two
toad, toed, towed
told, tolled

**V**

vain, vane, vein
vale, veil
vial, vile
vice, vise

**W**

wade, weighed
wail, whale
waist, waste
wait, weight
ware, wear, where
way, weigh, whey
weak, week
weather, whether
which, witch
while, wile
whine, wine
wood, would

**Y**

yoke, yolk
your, you're

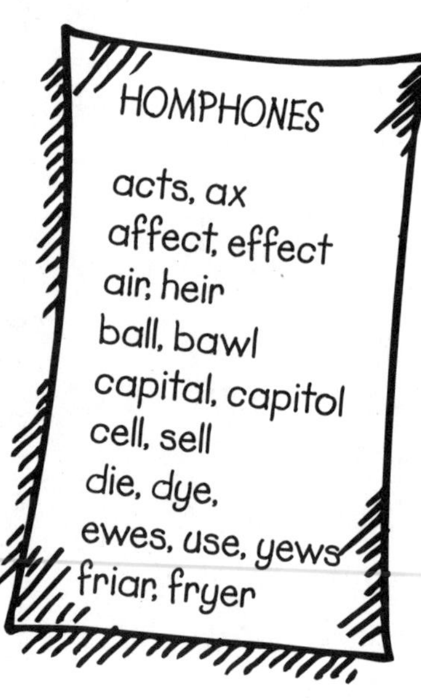

# SPELLING DEMONS

## Conquering Demons

On the following pages, you will find a list of spelling demons and other commonly misspelled words. Demons are words that sneak in an extra silent letter, contain unusual vowel or consonant combinations, have a homophone partner, or simply defy all concepts of phonetic logic!

To conquer spelling demons, some rote memorization is necessary. However, it is also very important to spend time analyzing each word to determine just what makes it so fiendishly difficult. The following can help your students master their personal troublemakers.

**Point out the trouble spot within the word.** For example:

calendar—the ending is ar, not er
dilemma—requires a double m, not just one
eighth—contains an unusual combination of consonants in the last four-letter sequence
doubt—has a silent letter b
fluorescent—has an unusual pairing of vowels because the u goes before the o

**Discuss which rule the demon is breaking.** For example:

caffeine—does not follow the i before e rule
dyeing—does not drop the final e before adding a suffix that begins with a vowel
judgment—does not follow the rule of retaining the final e before adding a suffix that begins with a consonant
subtly—does not retain the complete base word when adding the suffix ly

**Mispronunciation on the part of the speller may be the cause of confusion.** For example:

The word is:

pumpkin—not punkin
sandwich—not sanwich
Valentine—not Valentime
nuclear—not nuculer

**Determine if the word is from a foreign language and retains that spelling.** For example:

etiquette—French
memoir—French
kindergarten—German
spaghetti—Italian
cocoa—Spanish

**If the spelling of the word is extremely illogical, noticing its absurdity may help students remember it.** For example:

yacht—What is that c doing there? Remember it by thinking that on a yacht you take a cruise.
February—Who ever heard of a silent r? Mispronounce the word when trying to spell it—say Feb roo ary in your mind.
colonel—Can anyone explain this one? It is a really weird combination of French and Italian. It is also a tough one for which to create a mnemonic device. Try exaggerating the syllables: col O nel. Perhaps remembering that **colo**nels like their men to march in **col**umns will help correct spelling.

**Use other mnemonic devices to help aid mastery.** For example:

counsel**or** —the **or** reminds us of choice; a counselor helps us to make choices
aerial—**ae**rial stunts provide **a**ir **e**xcitement
friend—mispronounce the word in your mind: FRI end

There are many ways to work with spelling demons. For one, you may choose to use them as the entire list for the week. This is not recommended for younger children, but many advanced students in the upper grades will be able to cope with the challenge. Another option is to add one demon to each spelling list you present. Pick the demon according to the needs of your classroom. For example, most fourth graders will not find a great deal of usage for the word hypocrisy, but should master the spelling of Wednesday. Encourage sixth graders to increase their vocabulary by adding bizarre, inferior, and unique to their weekly lists. Remember to have students write any demons they are working with in the "PLUS" section of their logbooks.

# Spelling Demon List

**A**
abscess
absence
absolutely
accelerate
acceptance
accessible
accommodate
accumulation
accurate
ache
achievement
acknowledged
acquaintance
acquire
actual
actually
address
adequately
adjourned
admirable
adolescence
advantageous
advertise
advisable
aerial
again
aggravate
agreeable
alcohol
align
alleged
already
amateur
amendment
analysis
analyze
ancient
anecdote
annoyance
answer
antidote
anxious
apparatus
apparent
argument
arraignment
artificial
ascend
assessment
assistance
attendance

**B**
badminton
bankrupt
baptism
bargain
basis
beautiful
because
beige
beleaguered
believe
beneficial
biscuit
bizarre
bought
breath
breathe
bureau
bureaucracy
burglar
business

**C**
caffeine
calendar
campaign
canceled
captain
cashier
category
ceiling
cemetery
century
certainly
challenge
character
chief
chocolate
choir
Christmas
circuit
clothes
cocoa
collaborate
college
colonel
column
commission
committal
committee
community
comparative
compatible
competent
conceivable
condemn
confectionery
confidence
confidential
congratulate
conscience
conscientious
consequence
continuous
convenience
cooperate
correlation
correspondence
could
counselor
counterfeit
courageous
courtesy
criticism
crystallized
curiosity
currency
customary
customer

**D**
daily
deceive
decision
defendant
deferred
deficient
definitely
delicious
deluxe
democracy
dependent
derogatory
descend
design
desirable
despair

desperate
development
difference
dilapidated
dilemma
disappearance
disciple
discipline
disease
dissatisfied
distinguish
donor
doubt
drudgery
dyeing
dying

**E**

earnest
ecstasy
edible
efficiency
efficient
eighth
either
embarrass
eminent
emphasize
emphatically
encourage
endeavor
enormous
enough
enthusiasm
entirely
entrance
environment
especially
essential
etiquette
exaggerate
exceed
excerpt
exhilaration
existence
experiential
explanation
expression
exquisite
extraordinary
extremely

**F**

familiar
family
fascinated
fatigue
faucet
favorite
February
field
fiery
finally
financial
fluorescent
foreign
forfeit
formerly
fragile
friend
fulfill

**G**

gaiety
gaudy
gauge
generally
genius
genuine
glacier
government
governor
graduation
grammar
grief
grievous
grocery
guarantee
guard
guidance
guilty
gymnasium

**H**

handkerchief
hangar
happened
happiness
harassment
hearth
height
heir
heritage
hindrance
homicide
honor
hoping
humorous
hurriedly
hydraulic
hygiene
hymn
hypocrisy

**I**

ideally
illegible
imaginary
immediate
imminent
impartiality
incense
incongruous
inconvenience
independence
independent
indict
inferior
inflammable
influence
influential
initial
instead
insurance
intercede
intermittent
interpret
interrupt
irrelevant
irresistible
itinerary
its
it's

**J**

jealous
jeopardy
jewelry
journal
judgment
justice

**K**

kindergarten
kitchen
knew
know
knowledge
knowledgeable
knuckles

**L**

laboratory
lacquer
language
lawyer
league
leisure